Windows Vista
Configuration

Lab Manual

Windows Vista Configuration

Lab Manual

CRAIG ZACKER

WILEY

EXECUTIVE EDITOR   John Kane

SENIOR EDITOR   Gary Schwartz

DIRECTOR OF MARKETING AND SALES   Mitchell Beaton

PRODUCTION MANAGER   Micheline Frederick

DEVELOPMENT AND PRODUCTION   Custom Editorial Productions, Inc.

Wiley 200th Anniversary logo designed by: Richard J. Pacifico

To order books or for customer service please, call 1-800-CALL WILEY (225-5945).

ISBN 978-0470-11165-9
Printed in the United States of America

10 9 8 7 6 5 4 3 2

BRIEF CONTENTS

CONTENTS

LAB 1
CREATING A DUAL BOOT ENVIRONMENT

This lab contains the following exercises and activities:

Exercise 1.1   Running Upgrade Advisor

Exercise 1.2   Installing from Windows XP

Exercise 1.3   Installing from a DVD Disk

Lab Review   Questions

Lab Challenge   Creating a Partition

BEFORE YOU BEGIN

The classroom network consists of student workstations connected to a local area network. A classroom server, called Server01, is also connected to the classroom network. Server01 is running Windows Server 2003 and is the domain controller for a domain called contoso.com. Throughout the labs in this manual, you will be working with the same workstation on which you will install, configure, maintain, and troubleshoot Windows Vista.

Before you start this lab, see your instructor for the information needed to fill in the following table:

Student workstation name (Computer##)	
Password for workstation Administrator account	
Account name in CONTOSO domain (student##)	
Password for account name in CONTOSO domain	
Product key for Windows Vista distribution share	

Working with Lab Worksheets

Each lab in this manual requires that you answer questions, shoot screen shots, or perform other activities that you will document in a worksheet named for the lab, such as lab01_worksheet.doc. You will find these worksheets on your student CD. As you perform the exercises in each lab, open the appropriate worksheet file using WordPad, fill in the required information, and save the file to your student folder on the SERVER01 computer. Your instructor will examine these worksheet files to assess your performance. At the end of each lab, make sure that you save your fully completed worksheet file to the server and not to your local drive.

The procedure for opening and saving a worksheet file is as follows:

1. Click Start, and then click Run. The Run dialog box appears.

2. In the Open text box, browse your student CD to find the worksheet for this lab. Click Open and then click OK.

3. The worksheet document opens in WordPad.

4. Complete all questions in the worksheet.

5. In WordPad, choose Save As from the File menu. The Save As dialog box appears.

6. In the File Name text box, key **\\server01\students\student##\lab##_worksheet_*yourname*** (where student## contains your student number, lab## contains the number of the lab you're working on, and *yourname* is your last name).

SCENARIO

A client has a computer in her home on which Windows XP is installed. She is interesting in trying Windows Vista, but is hesitant to commit to it fully because she works from home part-time and doesn't want to jeopardize her productivity. When examining her computer, you notice that her hard drive has two partitions, neither of which is even half full. You propose to the client that it might be possible to install Vista on her computer in a dual boot environment. She would be able to run Windows XP and access her work applications and documents, but would also be able to run Windows Vista (although not at the same time). To do so, she would need to move all data from her second disk partition to the first partition so that the second one could hold Vista.

After completing this lab, you will be able to:

■ Run the Upgrade Advisor application

■ Recognize what happens when you install Windows Vista incorrectly

■ Install Windows Vista in a dual boot environment

■ Perform a clean installation of Windows Vista

Estimated lab time: 60–90 minutes

Exercise 1.1	Running Upgrade Advisor
Overview	In this exercise, you run the Windows Upgrade Advisor program on your client's computer to determine whether it is capable of running Windows Vista.
Completion time	20 minutes

1. Turn on the workstation.

2. Press Ctrl+Alt+Del. The *Log On To Windows* page appears.

3. In the User Name text box, key **Administrator**. In the Password text box, key the password for the Administrator account as supplied by your instructor. From the Log On To drop-down list, select the local workstation name (Computer##) and click OK.

4. Click Start, and then click Run. The Run dialog box appears.

5. In the Open text box, key **\\server01\UpgradeAdvisor\WindowsVistaUpgradeAdvisor.msi** and click OK.

6. The *Welcome To The Windows Vista Upgrade Advisor Setup Wizard* page appears.

7. Click Next to continue. The *License Agreement* page appears.

8. Select the I Agree radio button and click Next. The *Select Installation Folder* page appears.

9. Select the Create Desktop Shortcut radio button, if desired, and click Next. The *Installing Windows Upgrade Advisor* page appears as the wizard installs the program.

10. The *Installation Complete* page appears. Leave the Launch Windows Vista Upgrade Advisor checkbox selected and click Close.

11. The Upgrade Advisor program loads, and the *Welcome to Windows Vista Upgrade Advisor* page appears.

12. Click the Start Scan button. As it scans the hardware and the software on your computer, Upgrade Advisor displays information about different Windows Vista editions.

13. When the *Scan Complete* page appears, as shown in Figure 1-1, click the See Details button. A screen appears, specifying whether your computer is capable of running Windows Vista and, if so, recommending a specific edition.

Which Windows Vista edition is right for you?	Home Basic	Business	Home Premium	Ultimate
Most secure Windows ever with Windows Defender and Windows Firewall	✔	✔	✔	✔
Quickly find what you need with Instant Search and Windows Internet Explorer	✔	✔	✔	✔
Elegant Windows Aero™ desktop experience with Windows Flip 3D navigation		✔	✔	✔
Best choice for laptops with enhanced Windows Mobility Center and Tablet PC support		✔	✔	✔
Collaborate and share documents with Windows Meeting Space		✔	✔	✔
Experience photos and entertainment in your living room with Windows Media Center			✔	✔
Enjoy Windows Media Center on TVs throughout your home with Xbox 360™ and other devices			✔	✔
Protect against hardware failure with advanced business backup features		✔		✔
Business Networking and Remote Desktop for easier connectivity		✔		✔
Better protect your data against loss or theft with Windows BitLocker™ Drive Encryption				✔

Figure 1-1
The Windows Vista Upgrade Advisor's *Scan Complete* page

14. From your student CD, open the lab01_worksheet file in WordPad and answer the following questions.

Question 1	*According to Upgrade Advisor, is your workstation capable of running Windows Vista?*
Question 2	*Is your workstation capable of running Windows Aero? If not, why not?*
Question 3	*Are there any devices in the computer for which Upgrade Advisor could not find information? If so, which ones?*
Question 4	*Are there any applications on the computer that might cause compatibility issues with Windows Vista?*
Question 5	*Are there any application compatibility issues that could inhibit your plan to create a dual boot environment? Why or why not?*
Question 6	*Have you discovered anything that would prevent you from proceeding with your plan to create a dual boot environment on the computer?*

15. Take a screen shot of the page that specifies whether the computer can run Windows Vista by pressing Alt+Prt Scr, and then paste it into the lab01_worksheet file in the page provided by pressing Ctrl+V.

16. Save the worksheet file to your student folder on the SERVER01 server as lab01_worksheet_*yourname*, where *yourname* is your last name.

17. Log off of your workstation.

Exercise 1.2	Installing from Windows XP
Overview	Before beginning work on the computer, you asked your client to clear the second partition on the hard disk of all data by copying it to the first partition containing Windows XP. In this way, you can install Windows Vista to the second partition.
Completion time	20 minutes

1. Press Ctrl+Alt+Del. The *Log On To Windows* page appears.

2. Log on to the computer using the local Administrator account.

3. Open the Run dialog box and, in the Open text box, key **\\server01\VistaInstall\setup.exe** and click OK.

4. The *Install Windows* page appears.

5. Click Install Now. The *Get Important Updates For Installation* page appears.

6. Click Do Not Get The Latest Updates For Installation. The *Type Your Product Key For Activation* page appears.

7. In the Product Key text box, type the key code supplied by your instructor. Leave the Automatically Activate Windows When I'm Online checkbox selected unless your instructor tells you otherwise. Then, click Next to continue. The *Please Read The License Terms* page appears.

8. Select the I Accept The License Terms checkbox and click Next. The *Which Type Of Installation Do You Want?* page appears.

9. Click the Custom (Advanced) option. The *Where Do You Want To Install Windows?* page appears.

10. Open the lab01_worksheet_*yourname* file you created in Exercise 1.1 and answer the following questions.

Question 7	Why should you not select the Upgrade option in this particular scenario?
Question 8	True or False? The Upgrade option is activated on this page because you are running the Windows Vista installation program from a network share rather than a DVD.

11. Select the only entry in the partition table (Disk 0 Partion 1 [C:]) and click Next.

12. Answer the following questions in your lab01_worksheet_*yourname* file.

Question 9	Describe what happens next.
Question 10	Will continuing this procedure provide the client with a viable dual boot environment. Why or why not?
Question 11	At this point, you ask your client why there is only one partition in the table from which to choose. She informs you that she misunderstood your instructions to clear the second partition and deleted it after moving all of her files to the first partition. Is there any way to complete the dual boot installation at this time? Explain why or why not.

13. Click Cancel to close the message box, and then click the X (Close) button to cancel the installation.

14. When a message box appears asking you to confirm the cancellation, click Yes.

15. Answer the following questions in your lab01_worksheet_*yourname* file.

Question 12	What task must you perform before you can install Windows Vista in a dual boot environment? Specify two different methods for performing this task.
Question 13	Write out the steps for a procedure that will accomplish the task you described in your answer to the previous question, using only the materials that are currently available to you.

16. Perform the procedure that you detailed in Question 1–13.

17. Answer the following questions in your lab01_worksheet_*yourname* file.

Question 14	Did the procedure do what you expected it to do?
Question 15	Can you now proceed with the Windows Vista installation and have it successfully create a dual boot environment?

18. Stop. Show your procedure to your instructor before proceeding to the next exercise.

Exercise 1.3	Installing from a DVD Disk
Overview	Your client has supplied you with her Windows Vista installation disk, so you will now use that disk to perform the Windows Vista installation on the dual boot system. She has also informed you that she needs you to leave some unallocated space free on the hard disk, so you will use the installation program's disk tools to create the Windows Vista partition.
Completion time	20 minutes

1. Insert the Windows Vista installation disk into the computer's DVD drive and restart the system.

2. Press any key to boot from the DVD (if necessary). A progress indicator screen appears as Windows is loading files.

3. The computer switches to the Windows graphical interface, and the *Install Windows* page appears.

4. Click Next to accept the default values for the Language To Install, Time And Currency Format, and Keyboard Or Input Method settings. The *Windows Vista Install Now* page appears.

5. Click the Install Now button. The *Type Your Product Key For Activation* page appears.

6. In the Product Key text box, type the key code supplied by your instructor. Leave the Automatically Activate Windows When I'm Online checkbox selected unless your instructor tells you otherwise. Click Next to continue. The *Please Read The License Terms* page appears.

7. Select the I Accept The License Terms checkbox and click Next. The *Which Type Of Installation Do You Want?* page appears.

8. Open the lab01_worksheet_*yourname* file you created in Exercise 1.1 and answer the following question.

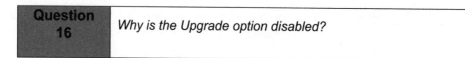

Question 16	*Why is the Upgrade option disabled?*

9. Click the Custom (Advanced) option. The *Where Do You Want To Install Windows?* page appears.

10. Click Drive Options (Advanced). Additional buttons appear on the page that you can use to manipulate the computer's disk partitions.

11. Select the partition you created in Exercise 1.2 (Disk 0 Partition 2) and click Delete. A message box appears, prompting you to confirm the deletion.

12. Click OK. The partition is removed from the list, and its space appears as Unallocated Space.

13. Select the Disk 0 Unallocated Space entry in the list and click New. A Size spin box appears.

14. In the Size spin box, key **30000** and click Apply. A new 30 GB partition appears in the list.

Question 17	What type of partition has the installation program created?
Question 18	Why are the disk tools in the installation program limited to creating primary partitions?

15. Select the partition you just created (Disk 0 Partion 2) and click Next. The *Installing Windows* page appears.

16. After several minutes during which the setup program installs Windows Vista, the computer reboots and the *Choose A User Name And Picture* page appears.

17. In the Type A User Name text box, enter **student##**.

18. In the Type A Password text box, enter the same password as the domain student## account supplied by your instructor, and repeat it in the Retype Your Password text box.

19. Click Next to continue. The *Type A Computer Name And Choose A Desktop Background* page appears.

20. In the Type A Computer Name checkbox, enter **computer##a** and click Next to continue. The *Help Protect Windows Automatically* page appears.

21. Select Ask Me Later. The *Review Your Time And Date Settings* page appears.

22. From the Time Zone drop-down list, select your time zone. If the date and time specified in the calendar and clock are not accurate, correct the settings and click Next. The *Select Your Computer's Current Location* page appears, as shown in Figure 1-2.

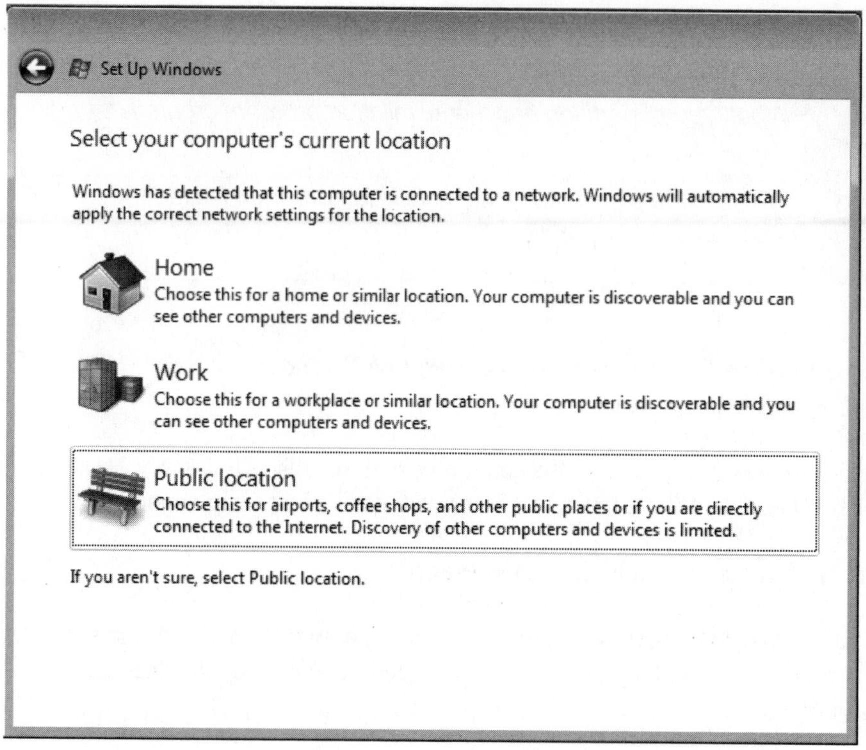

Figure 1-2
The *Select Your Computer's Current Location* page

23. Click Home. A *Thank You* page appears.

24. Click Start. The computer runs through a series of optimization routines as it starts Windows Vista for the first time. A few minutes later, the system completes its new startup routine and a logon window appears.

25. Log on as student##, using the password you specified. A *Preparing Your Desktop* page appears, followed by the Windows Vista desktop and the Welcome Center window.

26. Remove the Windows Vista installation disk from the DVD drive.

27. Click Start, click the arrow button in the lower right corner of the Start menu, and select Restart from the submenu.

28. Answer the following questions in your lab01_worksheet_*yourname* file.

Question 19	What happens when the computer restarts?
Question 20	What procedure should the client use to run Windows XP on the system?
Question 21	What tools can you use to modify the settings of the boot menu?

29. Save your worksheet file to your student## folder on SERVER01, and shut down your workstation.

LAB REVIEW QUESTIONS

Completion time   10 minutes

1. True or False? In Exercise 1.2, the Upgrade option is activated on the Which Type Of Installation Do You Want? page because you are running the Windows Vista installation program from a network share rather than a DVD.

2. In Exercise 1.3, why is the Upgrade option disabled?

3. What tools can you use to modify the settings of the boot menu that appears in Exercise 1.3?

LAB CHALLENGE: CREATING A PARTITION

Completion time   25 minutes

In Exercise 1.2, you wrote a procedure for creating a second partition on the computer's disk for the Windows Vista installation, using Windows XP tools. There are two Windows XP tools you can use to create the partition, a graphical tool and a command line tool. To complete this challenge, write a procedure to perform the same task with the tool you didn't use in Exercise 1.2. If you used the graphical tool earlier, use the command line tool here and vice versa.

LAB 2
USING WINDOWS EASY TRANSFER

This lab contains the following exercises and activities:

BEFORE YOU BEGIN

Lab 2 assumes that setup has been completed as specified in the setup document, that your workstation has connectivity to the classroom network and other lab computers, and that you have completed the exercises in Lab 1.

Before you start this lab, see your instructor for the information needed to fill in the following table:

Student workstation name (Computer##)	
Student account name (Student##)	

Working with Lab Worksheets

Each lab in this manual requires that you answer questions, shoot screen shots, or perform other activities that you will document in a worksheet named for the lab, such as lab01_worksheet.doc. You will find these worksheets on your student CD. As you perform the exercises in each lab, open the appropriate worksheet file using WordPad, fill in the required information, and save the file to your student folder on the SERVER01 computer. Your instructor will examine these worksheet files to assess your performance. At the end of each lab, make sure that you save your fully completed worksheet file to the server and not to your local drive.

The procedure for opening and saving a worksheet file is as follows:

1. Click Start, and then click Run. The Run dialog box appears.

2. In the Open text box, browse your student CD to find the worksheet for this lab. Click Open and then click OK.

3. The worksheet document opens in WordPad.

4. Complete all exercises in the worksheet.

5. In WordPad, choose Save As from the File menu. The Save As dialog box appears.

6. In the File Name text box, key **\\server01\students\student##\lab##_worksheet_*yourname*** (where student## contains your student number, lab## contains the number of the lab you're working on, and *yourname* is your last name).

SCENARIO

Your client is running Windows XP and Windows Vista in a dual boot environment. She originally installed Windows Vista to test the new operating system herself, but now her roomates, who share the computer, are interested in trying Vista as well. Your client wants to transfer her roomates' user accounts and documents from Windows XP to Windows Vista so that they can each log on using their own names. You explain to her that she can use the Windows Easy Transfer utility to do this.

In the Lab Challenge, you are asked to put yourself in the role of an administrator.

After completing this lab, you will be able to:

- Understand the components of a user profile

- Package Windows Easy Transfer for use on a Windows XP computer

- Take both a full and active window screen shot, and use Windows Easy Transfer to gather user profile information

- Use Windows Easy Transfer to migrate user profile information from one operating system to another

Estimated lab time: 120 minutes

Exercise 2.1	Creating User Profiles
Overview	In the following exercise, you create and populate additional user profiles on your Windows XP installation in preparation for transferring them to Windows Vista using Windows Easy Transfer.
Completion time	20 minutes

1. Turn on your workstation and, when the boot menu appears, select Previous Version of Windows. Windows XP starts and logs you on using the student## account.

2. Click Start, and then click Run. The Run dialog box appears.

3. In the Open text box, browse your student CD to find the worksheet for this lab. Click Open and then click OK. The worksheet document opens in WordPad.

4. In WordPad, choose File > Save As. The Save As dialog box appears.

5. Save a copy of the file to your My Documents folder.

6. Leave the lab02_worksheet file open in WordPad and answer the questions in the document as they appear in the lab.

Question 1	Where on the C: drive will you find the lab02_worksheet file you just saved?

7. Click Start, and then click Internet. An Internet Explorer window opens.

8. In the Address box, key **http://server01**. The classroom server's IIS default home page appears.

9. Click Favorites > Add To Favorites. The Add Favorite dialog box appears.

10. Click OK to add the page to the Favorites list.

11. Close the Internet Explorer window.

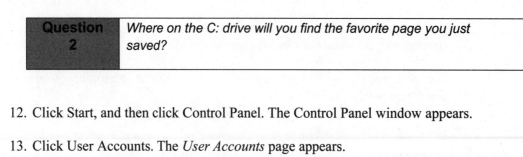

Question 2	Where on the C: drive will you find the favorite page you just saved?

12. Click Start, and then click Control Panel. The Control Panel window appears.

13. Click User Accounts. The *User Accounts* page appears.

14. Click Create A New Account. The *Name The New Account* page appears.

15. In the Type A Name For The New Account text box, key **Alice** and click Next. The *Pick An Account Type* page appears.

16. Select the Limited radio button and click Create Account. The Alice account appears on the *User Accounts* page.

17. Repeat Steps 14 to 16 to create three additional Limited user accounts called Ralph, Ed, and Trixie.

18. On the *User Accounts* page under Or Pick An Account To Change, click Alice. The *What Do You Want To Change About Alice's Account?* page appears.

19. Click Create A Password. The *Create A Password For Alice's Account* page appears.

20. In the Type A New Password and Type The New Password Again To Confirm text boxes, key **password** and click Create Password. The *What Do You Want To Change About Alice's Account?* page re-appears.

21. Click the Back button, and repeat Steps 18 to 20 to assign the password **password** to the Ralph account.

22. Click Start, and then click Log Off. The *Log Off Windows* page appears.

23. Click Log Off. The *To Begin, Click Your User Name* page appears.

24. Click Alice. In the Type Your Password text box, key **password** and click the Next button.

25. Repeat Steps 2 to 11 and log off.

26. Log on as Ed and repeat Steps 2 to 11.

27. Log off.

Exercise 2.2	Packaging Windows Easy Transfer
Overview	In the following exercise, you run Windows Easy Transfer on the Windows Vista computer and package the application to run at a later time on Windows XP.
Completion time	15 minutes

1. Restart the workstation and, when the boot menu appears, select Microsoft Windows Vista. Close the Welcome Center window.

2. Click Start, and then click Control Panel. The Control Panel window appears.

3. Click Network And Internet. The Network And Internet window appears.

4. Click Network And Sharing Center. The Network And Sharing Center window appears.

5. Under Sharing And Discovery, make sure that Network Discovery and File Sharing are turned on.

6. On the Windows Vista computer, click Start > All Programs > Accessories > System Tools and select Windows Easy Transfer. After you verify your credentials, the *Welcome To Windows Easy Transfer* page appears.

7. Click Next. The *Do You Want To Start A New Transfer Or Continue One In Progress?* page appears.

8. Click Start A New Transfer. The *Which Computer Are You Using Now?* page appears.

9. Click My New Computer. The *Do You Have An Easy Transfer Cable?* page appears.

10. Click No, Show Me More Options. The *Is Windows Easy Transfer Installed on Your Old Computer?* page appears.

11. Click No, I Need To Install It Now. The *Choose How to Install Windows Easy Transfer On Your Old Computer* page appears.

12. Click External Hard Disk Or Shared Network Folder. The *Choose An External Hard Disk Or Network Folder* page appears.

13. In the Enter A Location text box, click Browse and then navigate to the \\server01\students\student## folder.

14. Log on to Server01 using the account student## and the password **P@ssw0rd**, and then click Next.

15. The *Copying The Windows Easy Transfer Software* page appears as the wizard packages the software and copies it to the share. Afterward, the *Are Your Computers Connected To A Network?* page appears.

16. Click No, I Need To Use A CD, DVD, Or Other Removable Media. The *Copy Windows Easy Transfer To Your Old Computer* page appears.

17. Click Close, and then log off of Windows Vista.

Exercise 2.3	Collecting User Profile Data
Overview	In the following exercise, you run the Windows Easy Transfer program on Windows XP and collect the user profile data you want to migrate to Windows Vista.
Completion time	15 minutes

1. Restart the computer and, when the boot menu appears, select Earlier Version Of Windows to boot Windows XP.

2. Log on using the student## account.

3. Open the Run dialog box and, in the Open text box, key **\\server01\students\student##\MigWiz\MigSetup**. Click OK.

4. Log on to Server01 using the account name student## and the password **P@ssw0rd**.

5. The Windows Easy Transfer program loads, and the *Choose How To Transfer Files And Settings To Your New Computer* page appears.

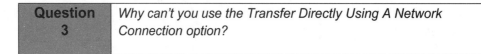

Question 3	*Why can't you use the Transfer Directly Using A Network Connection option?*

6. Click Use A CD, DVD, Or Other Removable Media. The *Choose How To Transfer File And Program Settings* page appears.

7. Click External Hard Disk Or To A Network Location. The *Choose A Network Location* page appears.

8. In the Network Location text box, key **\\server01\students\student##\transfer** and click Next. The *What Do You Want To Transfer To Your New Computer?* page appears.

9. Click Advanced Options. The *Select User Accounts, Files, And Settings To Transfer* page appears.

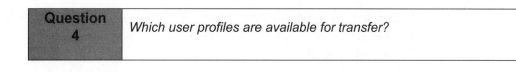

Question 4	Which user profiles are available for transfer?

10. Take a screen shot of the page displaying the user profiles on the system by pressing Ctrl+Prt Scr, and then paste it into the lab02_worksheet file in the page provided by pressing Ctrl+V.

11. Click Next to accept the default selections and begin the data collection process. When the process is completed, the *You're Ready To Transfer Files And Settings To Your New Computer* page appears.

12. Click Close. The Windows Easy Transfer application closes.

13. Log off of Windows XP.

Exercise 2.4   Importing User Profile Data

Overview	In the following exercise, you import the user profile data you collected in the previous exercise into Windows Vista.
Completion time	15 minutes

1. Restart the workstation and, when the boot menu appears, select Microsoft Windows Vista. Close the Welcome Center window.

2. On the Windows Vista computer, click Start > All Programs > Accessories > System Tools and select Windows Easy Transfer. After you verify your credentials, the *Welcome To Windows Easy Transfer* page appears.

3. Click Next. The *Do You Want To Start A New Transfer Or Continue One In Progress?* page appears.

4. Click Continue A Transfer In Progress. The *Are Your Computers Connected To A Network?* page appears.

5. Click No, I've Copied Files And Settings To A CD, DVD, Or Other Removable Media. The *Where Did You Save The Files And Settings You Want To Transfer?* page appears.

6. Click On An External Hard Disk Or Network Location. The *Where Did You Copy The Files And Settings You Want To Transfer?* page appears.

7. In the Enter The Path To Your Saved Data text box, key **\\server01\students\student##\transfer.mig** and click Next.

8. Log on to Server01 using the student## account and the password **P@ssw0rd** when you are prompted to do so. The *Type A New User Name Or Click A Name In The List* page appears.

9. For the Alice and Ed user accounts on the old computer, key the names **Alice** and **Ed** in the User Account On The New Computer text boxes and click Next. The *Select One Or More Drives To Use On Your New Computer* page appears.

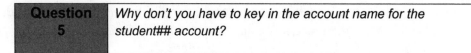

Question 5	Why don't you have to key in the account name for the student## account?

10. Click Next to accept the default drive assignments. The *Review Selected Files And Settings* page appears.

11. Click Transfer to begin the migration process. The *Please Wait Until The Transfer Is Complete* page appears.

12. When the migration process is complete, *The Transfer Is Complete* page appears, displaying a summary of the files and settings that were transferred.

13. Take a screen shot of the summary page by pressing Alt+Prt Scr, and then paste it into the lab02_worksheet file in the page provided by pressing Ctrl+V.

14. Click Show Me Everything That Was Transferred. A Windows Easy Transfer Report window appears.

15. Click Save. A Save As dialog box appears.

16. In the File Name text box, key **\\server01\students\student##\transferlog.htm** and click Save.

17. Log on to Server01 using the account student## and the password **P@ssw0rd**.

18. Click OK to close the Windows Easy Transfer Report window.

19. Click Close to exit the Windows Easy Transfer application. A message box appears, prompting you to restart the computer.

20. Click Yes to restart the computer.

Exercise 2.5	Testing User Profiles
Overview	In the following exercise, you examine the data that Windows Easy Transfer has migrated to Windows Vista and test the new user profiles that the application has created there.
Completion time	15 minutes

1. When the computer restarts, select Earlier Version Of Windows from the boot menu.

2. On Windows XP, log on using the Ed account.

Question 6	Is a password required? ~~No~~ *Yes*
Question 7	Is the lab02_worksheet file found in Ed's My Documents folder? *Yes*
Question 8	Is the Server01 shortcut found in Ed's Favorites folder? *No* ~~Yes~~

3. On Windows XP, log out of the Ed account and log on as Alice.

Question 9	Is a password required? *Yes*
Question 10	Is the lab02_worksheet file found in Alice's My Documents folder? *Yes*
Question 11	Is the Server01 shortcut found in Alice's Favorites folder? *No*

4. Restart the computer and, when the boot menu appears, select Microsoft Windows Vista.

5. On Windows Vista, log on using the Ed account, changing the password to **P@ssw0rd** when necessary.

Question 12	Is a password required?
Question 13	Is the lab02_worksheet file found in Ed's Documents folder?
Question 14	Is the Server01 shortcut found in Ed's Favorites folder?

6. On Windows Vista, log out of the Ed account and log on as Alice, changing the password to **P@ssw0rd** when necessary.

Question 15	Is a password required? No
Question 16	Is the lab02_worksheet file found in Alice's Documents folder?
Question 17	Is the Server01 shortcut found in Alice's Favorites folder?

LAB REVIEW QUESTIONS

Completion time	15 minutes

1. In Exercise 2.1, what other tool can you conceivably use to create and manage user accounts in Windows XP?

2. In Exercise 2.2, what would be the result if you failed to turn on the Network Discovery and File Sharing features?

3. In Exercise 2.3, why aren't the user profiles for all of the accounts you created available for transfer?

4. In Exercise 2.5, after you boot the system into Windows Vista, what accounts appear on the Welcome screen?

5. In Exercise 2.5, after booting into Windows Vista and logging on as Ed, where will you find the Windows Vista copy of the lab02_worksheet file you migrated?

6. In Exercise 2.5, after booting into Windows Vista, why don't you need to specify a password when logging on as Alice?

7. In Exercise 2.5, after booting into Windows Vista and logging on as Alice, where will you find the Windows Vista copy of the Server01 shortcut you just migrated?

LAB CHALLENGE: MIGRATING USER PROFILES OVER THE NETWORK

Completion time	25 minutes

You have been contracted to deploy a number of new computers for a small company. Each user is to receive a new computer running Windows Vista that will replace his or her old Windows XP computer. During the transition, both computers will be connected to the company network. Your task is to transfer the user profile settings from a Windows XP computer to a Windows Vista computer using a direct network connection in a side-by-side configuration.

Find a partner in the classroom and use your two computers to perform two side-by-side user profile migrations with the Windows Easy Transfer tool. For the first migration, you run Windows XP on your computer while your partner runs Windows Vista. Then, perform another migration with your computer running Windows Vista and your partner running Windows XP.

LAB 3
UPGRADING TO WINDOWS VISTA

This lab contains the following exercises and activities:

Exercise 3.1	Preparing to Upgrade
Exercise 3.2	Upgrading to Windows Vista
Exercise 3.3	Using the System Performance Rating Tool
Exercise 3.4	Customizing the Vista User Experience
Lab Review	Questions
Lab Challenge	Modifying Boot Configuration Data

BEFORE YOU BEGIN

Lab 3 assumes that setup has been completed as specified in the setup document, that your workstation has connectivity to the classroom network and other lab computers, and that you have completed the exercises in Labs 1 and 2.

Before you start this lab, see your instructor for the items and the information needed to fill in the following table:

Student workstation name (Computer##)	
Student account name (Student##)	
Product key for Windows Vista Distribution Share	
Windows Vista Installation Disk	

Working with Lab Worksheets

Each lab in this manual requires that you answer questions, shoot screen shots, or perform other activities that you will document in a worksheet named for the lab, such as lab01_worksheet.doc. You will find these worksheets on your student CD. As you perform the exercises in each lab, open the appropriate worksheet file using WordPad, fill in the required information, and save the file to your student folder on the SERVER01 computer. Your instructor will examine these worksheet files to assess your performance. At the end of each lab, make sure that you save your fully completed worksheet file to the server and not to your local drive.

The procedure for opening and saving a worksheet file is as follows:

1. Click Start, and then click Run. The Run dialog box appears.

2. In the Open text box, browse your student CD to find the worksheet for this lab. Click Open and then click OK.

3. The worksheet document opens in WordPad.

4. Complete all exercises in the worksheet.

5. In WordPad, choose Save As from the File menu. The Save As dialog box appears.

6. In the File Name text box, key **\\server01\students\student##\lab##_worksheet_***yourname*** (where student## contains your student number, lab## contains the number of the lab you're working on, and *yourname* is your last name).

SCENARIO

Your client is running Windows XP and Windows Vista in a dual boot environment. She originally wanted to install Windows Vista on a separate partition so that she could evaluate it. Now, having worked with Vista for a while, she is happy with the new operating system and wants to upgrade the Windows XP partition to Vista as well. This would provide her with two separate Vista installations, one of which she can use for testing new and potentially unstable products and the other for mission critical work.

After completing this lab, you will be able to:

- Prepare to perform a Windows Vista upgrade

- Upgrade a computer from Windows XP to Windows Vista

26

- Customize the Windows Vista user experience

- Run the System Performance Rating Tool

- Configure Windows Sidebar

Estimated lab time: 125 minutes

Exercise 3.1	Preparing to Upgrade
Overview	In the following exercise, you make final checks before upgrading to Windows Vista to ensure that there is enough disk space available, to print out a list of the installed device drivers, and to run Upgrade Advisor one final time.
Completion time	20 minutes

1. Turn on your workstation and, when the boot menu appears, select Previous Version Of Windows. Windows XP then starts.

2. Log on using the student## account.

3. Open the Run dialog box and browse your student CD to find the worksheet for this lab. Click Open and then click OK. The worksheet document opens in WordPad.

4. In WordPad, choose File > Save As. The Save As dialog box appears.

5. Save a copy of the file to the \\server01\students\student## folder.

6. Log on to Server01 using the student## account and the password **P@ssw0rd**.

7. Leave the lab03_worksheet file open in WordPad and answer the questions in the document as they appear in the lab. If you must restart the computer, be sure to reopen the copy of the worksheet on the Server01 server.

8. Open Windows Explorer and expand the My Computer heading.

Question 1	*To which drive will you be installing Windows Vista?*
Question 2	*How much free disk space is there on that drive?*
Question 3	*Is there enough space to install Window Vista?*

9. Click Start, and then click Control Panel. The Control Panel window appears.

10. Click Performance And Maintenance, and then click System. The System Properties dialog box appears.

11. Select the Hardware tab, and then click Device Manager. The Device Manager window opens.

12. Expand the Display Adapters heading, and double-click the display adapter beneath it. The Properties dialog box for the display adapter appears.

13. Click the Driver tab.

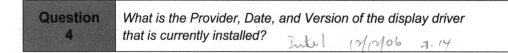

Question 4	What is the Provider, Date, and Version of the display driver that is currently installed? *Intel 17/17/06 7.14*

14. Take a screen shot of the Properties dialog box by pressing Ctrl+Prt Scr, and then paste it into the lab03_worksheet file in the page provided by pressing Ctrl+V.

15. Click OK to close the Properties dialog box.

16. In the Device Manager window, select Action > Print. The Print dialog box appears.

17. In the Select Printer box, select Microsoft XPS Document Writer. In the Report Type box, select All Devices And System Summary.

18. Click Print. A Save The File As dialog box appears.

19. In the File Name text box, key \\server01\students\student##\devicemanagerlog.xps and click Save.

20. Log on to Server01 using the account student## and the password P@ssw0rd.

21. When the printing process completes, close the devicemanagerlog window and the Device Manager window.

22. Run the Upgrade Advisor program one more time to make sure that the system is ready for an upgrade to Windows Vista.

NOTE	If necessary, refer to the instructions in Lab 1, "Creating a Dual Boot Environment," when running Upgrade Advisor.

23. Log off of the workstation.

Exercise 3.2	Upgrading to Windows Vista
Overview	In the following exercise, you upgrade your Windows XP workstation to Windows Vista.
Completion time	40 minutes

1. Restart your workstation and, when the boot menu appears, select Previous Version Of Windows. Windows XP starts.

2. Log on using the student## account.

3. Open the Run dialog box and, in the Open text box, key **\\server01\VistaInstall\Setup** and click OK.

4. Log on to Server01 using the student## account and the password **P@ssw0rd**.

5. The *Install Windows* screen appears.

6. Click Install Now. The *Get Important Updates For Installation* page appears.

7. Click Do Not Get The Latest Updates For Installation. The *Type Your Product Key For Activation* page appears.

8. In the Product Key text box, enter the product key supplied by your instructor and click Next. The *Please Read The License Terms* page appears.

9. Select the I Accept The License Terms checkbox and click Next. The *Which Type Of Installation Do You Want?* page appears.

10. Click Upgrade. After a compatibility check, a Compatibility Report screen appears, listing any problems or potential problems with the computer's hardware or software configuration.

11. Click Next. The *Upgrading Windows* page appears.

12. After a period that can last 30 minutes or more during which the setup program installs Windows Vista, the computer reboots. Allow the computer to boot to the default boot menu option, and the *Help Protect Windows Automatically* page eventually appears.

13. Click Ask Me Later. The *Review Your Time And Date Settings* page appears.

14. From the Time Zone drop-down list, select your time zone and, if necessary, correct the Date and Time settings. Click Next. The *Select Your Computer's Current Location* page appears.

15. Click the Work option. A *Thank You* page appears.

16. Click Start. The computer runs through a series of optimization routines as it starts Windows Vista for the first time. A Preparing Your Desktop screen appears.

17. A few minutes later, the system completes its new startup routine and the Welcome Center window appears.

18. Shut down the computer.

Exercise 3.3	Using the System Performance Rating Tool
Overview	In the following exercise, you use the System Performance Rating Tool to determine your computer's base score.
Completion time	15 minutes

1. Turn on your workstation and, when the boot menu appears, select the default (first) Microsoft Windows Vista entry.

2. When Windows Vista starts, log on using the student## account.

3. In the upper right corner of the Welcome Center window, click Show More Details. The *View Basic Information About Your Computer* page appears.

4. In the System section, click Windows Experience Index. The *Rate And Improve Your Computer's Performance* page appears.

Question 5	What is the base score for your computer?	3.5
Question 6	Which of the system's components is responsible for creating the base score? *Processor, RAM, Graphics, Gaming Gn HDP*	
Question 7	What can you do to increase your computer's base score? *Graphics, RAM Processor*	

5. Take a screen shot of the *Rate And Improve Your Computer's Performance* page by pressing Ctrl+Prt Scr, and then paste it into the lab03_worksheet file in the page provided by pressing Ctrl+V.

6. Log off and turn off the computer.

Exercise 3.4	Customizing the Vista User Experience
Overview	In the following exercise, you modify the appearance of the Start menu.
Completion time	15 minutes

1. Turn on your workstation and, when the boot menu appears, select the default (first) Microsoft Windows Vista entry.

2. When Windows Vista starts, log on using the student## account.

3. Close the Welcome Center window.

4. Right-click the Start button and, from the context menu, select Properties. The Taskbar and Start Menu Properties dialog box appears.

5. On the Start Menu tab, with the Start Menu radio button selected, click the Customize button. The Customize Start Menu dialog box appears.

6. Under Control Panel, select the Display As A Menu radio button.

Question 8	How does it benefit the desktop technician to display the Control Panel as a menu?

7. In the Start Menu Size box, change the Number Of Recent Programs To Display value to 15 and click OK.

8. Click OK to close the Taskbar and Start Menu Properties dialog box.

9. Click Start > All Programs > Accessories, right-click Windows Explorer and, from the context menu, select Pin To Start Menu. The Windows Explorer shortcut appears in the pinned area of the Start menu.

10. Log off and turn off the computer.

LAB REVIEW QUESTIONS

Completion time	10 minutes

1. In Exercise 3.1, assuming that Upgrade Advisor found your workstation suitable for a Windows Vista installation in Lab 1, what could possibly have changed between now and then to prevent you from upgrading to Windows Vista?

2. In Exercise 3.2, why do the student##, Alice, and Ed user accounts appear on the Welcome screen of Windows Vista?

3. Once you finish performing the upgrade described in Exercise 3.2 and boot into the newly installed copy of Windows Vista, the operating system files are located in the C:\Windows folder. When you restart the system and select the other copy of Windows Vista from the boot menu, where will you find the operating system files?

4. Why does the System Performance Rating Tool use the lowest component score to determine the base score for the computer?

LAB CHALLENGE: MODIFYING BOOT CONFIGURATION DATA

Completion time	25 minutes

After upgrading the Windows XP partition on your client's computer to Windows Vista, she is left with a confusing boot menu that lists two identical instances of Microsoft Windows Vista as its boot options. Currently, the first Microsoft Windows Vista boot option, which is the default, is the upgrade you just performed that uses the computer name computer##. The second Microsoft Windows Vista boot option is the clean installation you performed in Lab 1 that uses the computer name computer##a.

Your task in this challenge is to modify the boot menu so that the two boot menu options read as follows:

- Windows Vista – Upgrade – Computer##
- Windows Vista – Clean – Computer##a

Unlike Windows XP, which stores its boot menu data in a configuration file called Boot.ini, Windows Vista uses a new boot configuration system called Boot Configuration Data (BCD). To work with the BCD, you use a command line program called Bcdedit.exe. Because the BCD is in use when Windows Vista is running, you must run Bcdedit.exe from the Windows Recovery Environment (Windows RE).

To access Windows RE, you must boot the computer from a Windows Vista installation disk, click Repair Your Computer, click Next, and then choose the Command Prompt option. From this command prompt, you can run Bcdedit.exe and access both the live boot configuration data for the system and the program's context-sensitive help system, which you can use to determine the correct syntax for your commands.

	You will use the Bcdedit.exe program with the /set parameter to perform your modifications.

In your lab03_worksheet file, specify the Bcdedit commands you must use to make the modifications specified earlier in this challenge. After you have written out your commands, execute them on your workstation and test your results by restarting the computer and checking the boot menu entries.

Question 9	*What command will modify the first boot menu option to read "Microsoft Windows Vista – Upgrade – Computer##" (where ## is the number of your workstation)?*
Question 10	*What command will modify the first boot menu option to read "Microsoft Windows Vista – Clean – Computer##a" (where ## is the number of your workstation)?*

LAB 4
WORKING WITH DISKS

This lab contains the following exercises and activities:

Exercise 4.1   Creating a Basic Disk Partition

Exercise 4.2   Extending a Basic Disk Partition

Exercise 4.3   Creating Additional Partitions

Exercise 4.4   Mounting a Volume

Exercise 4.5   Working with Dynamic Disks

Lab Review   Questions

Lab Challenge   Backing Up

BEFORE YOU BEGIN

Lab 4 assumes that setup has been completed as specified in the setup document, that your workstation has connectivity to the classroom network and other lab computers, and that you have completed the exercises in Labs 1 to 3. At this point, there should be two copies of Windows Vista installed on the student workstation, one clean installation that you performed in Lab 1 and one upgrade that you performed in Lab 3. There should also be 20 gigabytes of unallocated space on the workstation's hard disk.

Before you start this lab, make sure you have the following information for your workstation:

Student workstation name (Computer##)	
Student account name (Student##)	

Working with Lab Worksheets

Each lab in this manual requires that you answer questions, shoot screen shots, or perform other activities that you will document in a worksheet named for the lab, such as Lab01_worksheet.doc. You will find these worksheets on your student CD. As you perform the exercises in each lab, open the appropriate worksheet file using WordPad, fill in the required information, and save the file to your student folder on the SERVER01 computer. Your instructor will examine these worksheet files to assess your performance. At the end of each lab, make sure that you save your fully completed worksheet file to the server and not to your local drive.

The procedure for opening and saving a worksheet file is as follows:

1. Click Start, and then click Run. The Run dialog box appears.

2. In the Open text box, browse your student CD to find the worksheet for this lab. Click Open and then click OK.

3. The worksheet document opens in WordPad.

4. Complete all exercises in the worksheet.

5. In WordPad, choose Save As from the File menu. The Save As dialog box appears.

6. In the File Name text box, key **\\server01\students\student##\lab##_worksheet_*yourname*** (where student## contains your student number, lab## contains the number of the lab you're working on, and *yourname* is your last name).

SCENARIO

You are a desktop technician working at the help desk in a medium-sized organization. One morning, a user named Alice calls and complains that she created an important document file for her boss yesterday, saved it to her hard drive, and now cannot find it. Alice goes on to explain that this sort of thing happens to her all the time: she creates files and saves them, and when she tries to open them again, she must spend half an hour looking for them. Sometimes she finds the file she needs and sometimes she doesn't, which forces her to create it all over again.

When you examine Alice's hard disk, you find document files strewn about the drive everywhere, with some intermixed with application files and others stored in the root of the drive. You decide to show Alice the basics of file management, starting with how to create a new partition for her data and thereby keep it separate from her application and operating system files.

After completing this lab, you will be able to:

- Create a basic primary partition

- Create an extended partition and logical drives

- Convert a basic disk to a dynamic disk

- Create dynamic disk volumes

- Extend and shrink dynamic volumes

- Mount a volume in an NTFS folder

Estimated lab time: 125 minutes

Exercise 4.1	Creating a Basic Disk Partition
Overview	Thanks to your instruction, Alice now sees the advantage to storing her data files on a partition separate from the operating system and application files. In the following exercise, you create a new basic partition for her where she can store her data.
Completion time	20 minutes

1. Turn on your workstation and, when the boot menu appears, select the clean copy of Windows Vista you installed in Lab 1.

2. Log on to the local machine using the student## account.

3. Open the Run dialog box and browse your student CD to find the worksheet for this lab. Click Open and then click OK. The worksheet document opens in WordPad.

4. In WordPad, choose File > Save As. The Save As dialog box appears.

5. Save a copy of the file to the \\server01\students\student## folder.

6. When prompted, log on to Server01 using the student## account and the password **P@ssw0rd**.

7. Leave the lab04_worksheet file open in WordPad and answer the questions in the document as they appear in the lab. If you have to restart the computer, be sure to reopen the copy of the worksheet on the Server01 server.

8. Click Start, and then click Control Panel. The Control Panel window appears.

9. Click System And Maintenance, and then click Administrative Tools. The Administrative Tools window appears.

10. Double-click the Computer Management shortcut. Click Continue to confirm that you are performing the task. The Computer Management console appears.

11. In the scope (left) pane, click Disk Management. The Disk Management snap-in appears in the details pane.

12. Based on the information in the Disk Management snap-in, fill out the information in Table 4-1 on your lab worksheet.

Table 4-1
Disk information

	Disk 0
Disk type (basic or dynamic)	
Total disk size	
Number and type of partitions	
Amount of unallocated space	

 NOTE | *If there is not at least one gigabyte of unallocated space available on your workstation, see your instructor before you continue.*

13. In the graphical display in the bottom view pane, select the Unallocated area of Disk 0. On the Action menu, point to All Tasks and select New Simple Volume. The New Simple Volume Wizard appears.

14. Click Next to bypass the *Welcome* page. The *Specify Volume Size* page appears.

15. In the Simple Volume Size In MB text box, key **2000** and click Next. The *Assign Drive Letter Or Path* page appears.

16. Leave the Assign The Following Drive Letter radio button selected, and then choose drive letter X from the drop-down list and click Next. The *Format Partition* page appears.

17. Leave the Format This Partition With The Following Settings radio button selected, and configure the next three parameters as follows:

   - File System: FAT32

- Allocation Unit Size: Default

- Volume Label: Alice1

18. Select the Perform A Quick Format checkbox and click Next. The *Completing The New Simple Volume Wizard* page appears.

19. Click Finish. The new Data partition appears in the Disk Management snap-in and an Explorer window appears, showing the contents of the X: drive.

20. Leave the Computer Management console open for future exercises.

Exercise 4.2	Extending a Basic Disk Partition
Overview	A few days later, you receive another call at the help desk from Alice. She has been diligently moving her data files to the special partition you created for her, but she has now run out of disk space. The partition was not big enough! To address the problem, you decide to extend the Alice1 partition, using some of the unallocated space left on the disk. For this task, you intend to use the Diskpart.exe command line utility.
Completion time	20 minutes

1. On Computer*x##x*,a, click Start, point to All Programs > Accessories, and open Windows Explorer.

2. In the Folders pane, expand the Computer container and locate the X: drive you created in Exercise 4.1.

3. Right-click the X: drive and, from the context menu, select New > Folder. Give the new folder the name **Vista**.

4. Expand the Network container, expand Server01, and select the VistaInstall share.

5. Copy all files and folders from the VistaInstall share to the X:\Vista folder you created.

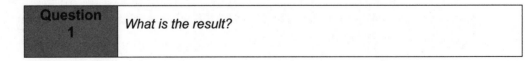

Question 1	What is the result?

6. Click Cancel.

7. Consult the Disk Management snap-in, and fill out the following table with the amount of unallocated space left on the drive in gigabytes and megabytes.

Table 4-2
Unallocated space remaining

	Disk 0
Unallocated space left (in gigabytes)	
Unallocated space left (in megabytes)	

8. Click Start, point to All Programs > Accessories, and click Command Prompt. A Command Prompt window appears.

9. In the Command Prompt window, key **diskpart** and press Enter. Click Continue to confirm that you are performing the task, and a new window with DISKPART> prompt appears.

10. Key **select disk 0** and press Enter. The program responds, saying that disk 0 is now the selected disk.

11. Key **list partition** and press Enter. A list of the partitions on disk 0 appears.

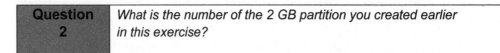

Question 2	What is the number of the 2 GB partition you created earlier in this exercise?

12. Key **select partition #**, where # is the number of the 2 GB partition, and press Enter. The program responds, saying that partition 3 is now the selected partition.

13. Key **extend size=xxxx**, where xxxx is the amount of unallocated space left on the drive in megabytes from Table 4-1, and press Enter.

Question 3	Why does the command not execute properly?

14. Key **exit** and press Enter. The DISKPART window closes, returning you to the standard command prompt.

15. At the command prompt, key **convert x: /fs:ntfs /v /x** and press Enter.

Question 4	What happens?

16. Click Start, point to All Programs > Accessories, right-click Command Prompt and, from the context menu, select Run As Administrator. Click Allow to confirm that you are performing the task, and another Command Prompt window appears.

17. Repeat the Convert.exe command from Step 15. When the program prompts you for the volume label for drive X:, key **Alice1** and press Enter.

Question 5	What happens now?

18. Run the Diskpart.exe program again and repeat the commands from steps 10 through 13.

Question 6	What is the result?

19. Key **exit** and press Enter to terminate the Diskpart program.

20. Try again to copy the contents of the VistaInstall share to the X:\Vista folder.

Question 7	What is the result?

21. Leave the computer logged on for the next exercise.

Exercise 4.3	Creating Additional Partitions
Overview	Alice is thrilled at the idea of storing her data files in separate partitions, and now she wants you to create more partitions on her drive. However, you use all of the available space to create her Alice1 partition. Therefore, you must shrink the Alice1 partition to create room for the additional partitions that she wants.
Completion time	20 minutes

1. On Computer## a in the Disk Administrator snap-in, right-click the Data volume you created on Disk 0 and, from the context menu, select Shrink Volume. The Shrink X: dialog box appears.

Question 8	How much available shrink space can be found in the volume?

2. In the Enter The Amount Of Space To Shrink spin box, key the amount of available shrink space minus 2000 MB (2 GB).

3. Click Shrink. The amount of space you entered appears as unallocated space in the Disk Management snap-in.

4. Right-click the unallocated space and select New Simple Volume. The New Simple Volume Wizard appears.

5. Use the wizard to create a new 2000 MB partition using the drive letter Y:, the NTFS file system, and the volume name Alice2.

Question 9	How is the resulting volume different from the one you created in Exercise 4.1? Explain why..
Question 10	What do you suppose would happen if you created another simple volume out of the free space left on the disk?

6. Take a screen shot of the Disk Management snap-in that shows the volumes you created by pressing Ctrl+Prt Scr, and then paste the resulting image into the lab04_worksheet file in the page provided by pressing Ctrl+V.

7. Leave the Computer Management console open for the next exercise.

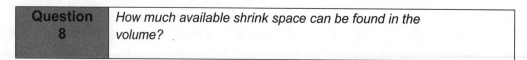

Exercise 4.4	Mounting a Volume
Overview	Alice calls the help desk yet again to tell you that she needs still more space on her Alice1 partition, but is unable to expand it. You decide to provide her with additional space by creating a volume and mounting it in a folder on the Alice1 volume.
Completion time	20 minutes

1. In the Disk Management snap-in, right-click the Alice1 volume you created in Exercise 4.1 and try to extend it by 2000 MB.

Question 11	Were you successful?

2. Now right-click the Alice2 volume you created in Exercise 4.3 and try to extend it by 2000 MB.

Question 12	Were you successful?

3. On Computer##a, open Windows Explorer and create a new folder on the computer's X: drive called Alice3.

4. In the Disk Management snap-in, right-click the remaining Free Space element on Disk 0 and, from the context menu, select New Simple Volume.

5. In the New Simple Volume Wizard, specify a volume size of 2000 MB.

6. On the *Assign Drive Letter Or Path* page, select the Mount In The Following Empty NTFS Folder radio button. In the text box, key **X:\Alice3** and click Next.

7. On the *Format Partition* page, select the NTFS file system and assign the volume the label Alice3.

8. Click Next and click Finish to create the volume.

9. Open Windows Explorer, right-click the X: drive, and open its Properties sheet.

Question 13	According to Windows Explorer, what is the capacity of the X: drive?
Question 14	Does the capacity shown for the X: drive in Windows Explorer reflect the addition of the mounted volume?

10. Select the Alice3 icon.

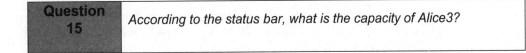

Question 15	According to the status bar, what is the capacity of Alice3?

> **NOTE**   *If the status bar does not appear at the bottom of the Windows Explorer window, activate it by selecting Status Bar from the View menu.*

11. Leave the Computer Management console open for the next exercise.

Exercise 4.5	Working with Dynamic Disks
Overview	Alice currently has five partitions on her basic disk: three primary partitions and one extended partition with two logical drives. She has found it difficult to manage her files with so many partitions, so she wants to consolidate the disk into just three volumes—her original two plus one large data volume—that will be part of a striped volume. Unfortunately, the second hard disk drive for Alice's computer is back-ordered, so you cannot create the stripe set yet. However, you are going to prepare for the upgrade by converting the basic disk to a dynamic disk and consolidating the partitions. Alice has already copied all of her files from the Alice2 and Alice3 volumes to Alice1.
Completion time	20 minutes

1. In the Disk Management snap-in, in the graphical display, right-click the Disk 0 box and, from the context menu, select Convert To Dynamic Disk. The Convert To Dynamic Disk dialog box appears.

2. Leave the default Disk 0 checkbox selected and click OK. The Disks To Convert dialog box appears.

3. Click Convert. A Disk Management message box appears, warning you that after you convert the disk to a dynamic disk, you will not be able to start other operating systems in a dual boot arrangement.

4. Click Yes to continue. The snap-in performs the disk conversion.

Question 16	What has happened to the primary partitions and logical drives that you created earlier in this lab?

5. Take a screen shot of the Disk Management snap-in that shows the dynamic volumes you created by pressing Ctrl+Prt Scr, and then paste the resulting image into the lab04_worksheet file in the page provided by pressing Ctrl+V.

6. Right-click the Alice3 volume and, from the context menu, select Delete Volume. A Delete Simple Volume dialog box appears.

7. Click Yes to confirm that you want to delete the volume. The Alice3 volume reverts to unallocated space.

8. Delete the Alice2 volume using the same procedure.

9. Right-click the Alice1 volume and, from the context menu, select Extend Volume. The Extend Volume Wizard appears.

10. Using the wizard, extend the volume using all of the remaining unallocated space on the disk.

11. Close the Computer Management console and log off of the computer.

LAB REVIEW QUESTIONS

Completion time	10 minutes

1. In Exercise 4.3, why doesn't the extended partition that you created appear in the Disk Management snap-in's volume list in the top view pane?

2. In Exercise 4.4, why were you unable to extend the Alice1 volume and forced to mount a volume to a folder instead, but were able to extend Alice2?

3. In Exercise 4.5, after you converted the basic disk to a dynamic disk, how many partitions can be found on the disk? How do you know?

4. If, after creating a spanned volume containing space from three hard disks, one of the hard disk drives fails, what happens to the data stored on the volume?

LAB CHALLENGE: BACKING UP

Completion time	25 minutes

While working on Alice's computer, you discover that she is not backing up her data in any way. After explaining the need for regular backups to her, you proceed to configure her computer to perform weekly backups of her data files and her entire system drive. To complete this challenge, create two backup schedules on your workstation: one using the Backup Files Wizard to back up all of your document files and one using Complete PC to back up your C: drive. Use the Alice1 volume you created as the target for both jobs, and configure the document backup to repeat weekly.

Take a screen shot of the Backup And Restore Center that shows the dates and times of the completed backup jobs by pressing Ctrl+Prt Scr, and then paste the resulting image into the lab04_worksheet file in the page provided by pressing Ctrl+V.

LAB 5
WORKING WITH USERS AND GROUPS

This lab contains the following exercises and activities:

Exercise 5.1　　Modifying Account and Password Policies

Exercise 5.2　　Creating Local Users

Exercise 5.3　　Using the Local Users And Groups Snap-in

Exercise 5.4　　Managing Group Memberships

Exercise 5.5　　Configuring Logon Behavior

Lab Review　　Questions

Lab Challenge　　Using Net.exe

BEFORE YOU BEGIN

Lab 5 assumes that setup has been completed as specified in the setup document, that your workstation has connectivity to the classroom network and other lab computers, and that you have completed the exercises in Labs 1 to 4. At this point, there should be two copies of Windows Vista installed on the student workstation, one clean installation that you performed in Lab 1 and one upgrade that you performed in Lab 3.

Before you start this lab, make sure you have the following information for your workstation:

Student workstation name (Computer##)	
Student account name (Student##)	

Working with Lab Worksheets

Each lab in this manual requires that you answer questions, shoot screen shots, or perform other activities that you will document in a worksheet named for the lab, such as lab01_worksheet.doc. You will find these worksheets on your student CD. As you perform the exercises in each lab, open the appropriate worksheet file using WordPad, fill in the required information, and save the file to your student folder on the SERVER01 computer. Your instructor will examine these worksheet files to assess your performance. At the end of each lab, make sure that you save your fully completed worksheet file to the server and not to your local drive.

The procedure for opening and saving a worksheet file is as follows:

1. Click Start, and then click Run. The Run dialog box appears.

2. In the Open text box, browse your student CD to find the worksheet for this lab. Click Open and then click OK.

3. The worksheet document opens in WordPad.

4. Complete all exercises in the worksheet.

5. In WordPad, choose Save As from the File menu. The Save As dialog box appears.

6. In the File Name text box, key **\\server01\students\student##\lab##_worksheet_*yourname*** (where student## contains your student number, lab## contains the number of the lab you're working on, and *yourname* is your last name).

SCENARIO

You are a Windows Vista desktop support technician for Contoso, Ltd., a company with workstations in a variety of different environments. Some of the Windows Vista computers are members of a workgroup, while others are members of an Active Directory domain. You have been assigned the task of creating user and group accounts for new employees that the company has recently hired and assigning them the privileges they need to access various company resources. Because of the differing system configurations, the procedures for creating the users and groups vary.

After completing this lab, you will be able to:

- Modify default logon policies

- Create local user accounts

48

■ Create local groups

■ Manage group memberships

Estimated lab time: 125 minutes

Exercise 5.1	Modifying Account and Password Policies
Overview	The computers for the users in the Accounting department at Contoso, Ltd. are not members of the corporate domain. The IT director has decided that, for security reasons, these computers should be members of a separate workgroup, with each computer responsible for its own user authentication and access control. Several of the new hires will be working in the Accounting department, so you must configure their computers and create local user and group accounts on them. To maintain a secure environment, you are first going to modify the default account and password policies for a workgroup computer.
Completion time	20 minutes

1. Turn on your workstation and, when the boot menu appears, select the clean copy of Windows Vista you installed in Lab 1.

2. Log on to the local machine using the student## account.

3. Open the Run dialog box and browse your student CD to find the worksheet for this lab. Click Open and then click OK. The worksheet document opens in WordPad.

4. In WordPad, choose File > Save As. The Save As dialog box appears.

5. Save a copy of the file to the \\server01\students\student## folder.

6. When prompted, log on to Server01 using the student## account and the password **P@ssw0rd**.

7. Leave the lab05_worksheet file open in WordPad and answer the questions in the document as they appear in the lab. If you must restart the computer, be sure to reopen the copy of the worksheet on the Server01 server.

8. Click Start, and then click Control Panel > System And Maintenance > Administrative Tools. The Administrative Tools window appears.

9. Double-click Local Security Policy. After you confirm that you have performed the action, the Local Security Policy console appears.

10. Expand the Account Policies node, and click Password Policy. The default password policies appear in the details panel, as shown in Figure 5-1.

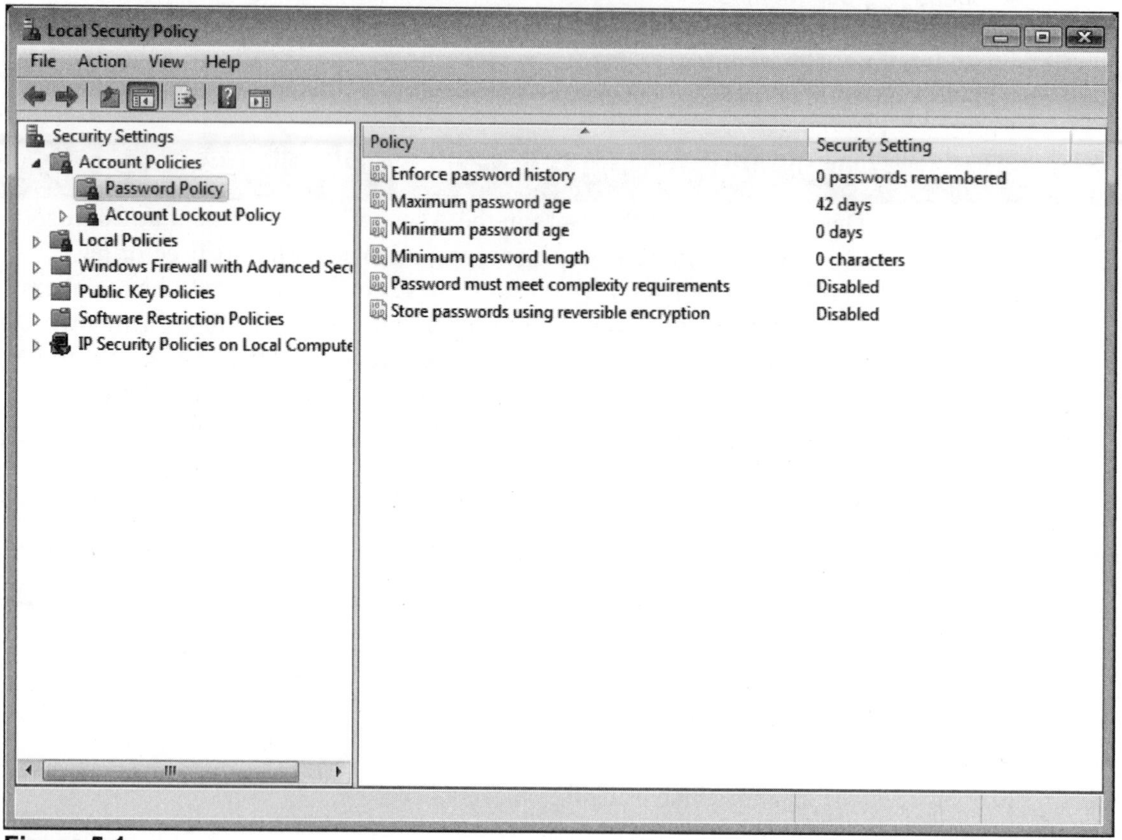

Figure 5-1
Default Windows Vista password policy settings

11. In Table 5-1 on your worksheet, record the workstation's current password policy settings.

Table 5-1
Windows Vista password policy defaults

Password Policy	Value
Enforce Password History	
Maximum Password Age	
Minimum Password Age	
Minimum Password Length	
Password Must Meet Complexity Requirements	
Store Passwords Using Reversible Encryption	

12. Double-click the Enforce Password History policy. The Enforce Password History dialog box appears.

13. Change the value of the policy to 24, and then click OK.

14. Double-click the Maximum Password Age policy, change the value to 7, and then click OK.

Question 1	How does reducing the Maximum Password Age value increase the security of the network?

15. Double-click the Minimum Password Age policy, change the value to 6, and then click OK.

16. Double-click the Minimum Password Length policy, change the value to 8, and then click OK.

17. Double-click the Password Must Meet Complexity Requirements policy, set the value to Enabled, and then click OK.

18. Take a screen shot of the Local Security Policy console with your new password policy settings displayed by pressing Ctrl+Prt Scr, and then paste the resulting image into the lab05_worksheet file in the page provided by pressing Ctrl+V.

19. In the console's scope pane, click the Account Lockout Policy node. The default account lockout policies appear in the details panel, as shown in Figure 5-2.

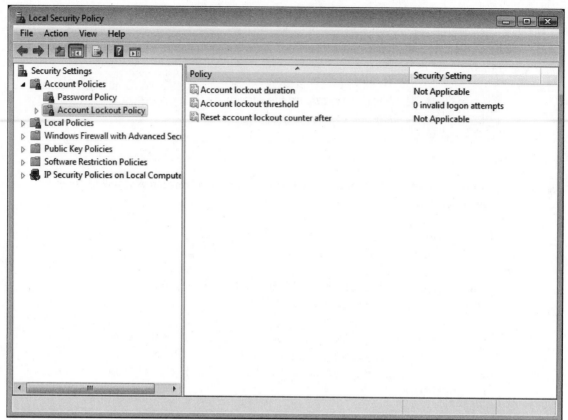

Figure 5-2
Default Windows Vista account lockout policy settings

20. In Table 5-2 on your worksheet, record the workstation's current password account lockout settings.

Table 5-2
Windows Vista account lockout policy defaults

Password Policy	Value
Account Lockout Duration	
Account Lockout Threshold	
Reset Account Lockout Counter After	

21. Double-click the Account Lockout Threshold policy, and change the value to 3 invalid logon attempts.

22. Click OK. A Suggested Value Changes dialog box appears.

23. Click OK to accept the default settings.

24. Double-click the Account Lockout Duration policy, and change the value to 10 minutes.

25. Double-click the Reset Account Lockout Counter After policy, and change the value to 3 minutes.

Question 2	After attempting to log on twice and failing, how long must you wait before a third failed logon attempt will not lock up the account?

26. Take a screen shot of the Local Security Policy console with your new account lockout policy settings displayed by pressing Ctrl+Prt Scr, and then paste the resulting image into the lab05_worksheet file in the page provided by pressing Ctrl+V.

27. Close the Local Security Policy console, and leave the computer logged on for the next exercise.

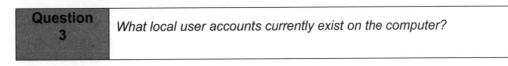

Exercise 5.2   Creating Local Users

Overview	The new hires in the Accounting department at Contoso, Ltd. need local user accounts for their workgroup computers—not only for themselves, but also for other department workers who need access to their data. In this exercise, you create a new local user account for the Director of the Accounting department, Jay Adams, using the Windows Vista User Accounts control panel.
Completion time	20 minutes

1. On your student workstation, click Start > Control Panel > User Accounts > User Accounts. The User Accounts window appears.

2. Click Manage Another Account. The Choose The User Account You Would Like To Change window appears.

Question 3	What local user accounts currently exist on the computer?

3. Click Create A New Account. The *Name The Account And Choose An Account Type* page appears.

4. In the New Account Name text box, key **JAdams**. Leave the Standard User radio button selected, and click Create User. The JAdams account is added to the Choose The User Account You Would Like To Change window.

5. Click the JAdams account you just created. The *Make Changes To JAdam's Account* page appears.

6. Click Change The Password. The *Change JAdams's Password* page appears.

7. In the New Password and Confirm New Password text boxes, key **pass** and click Change Password.

8. A User Account Control Panel message box appears, informing you that the password you keyed does not meet password policy requirements.

9. Click OK to continue.

Question 4	In what way(s) did the password you tried to use not meet the password policy requirements?

10. Try to set the password for the JAdams account using the passwords in Table 5-3. For each password that fails, explain why it failed in the space provided in your worksheet.

Table 5-3
Proposed passwords

Password	Reason for Failure
smadaj	
jadams000	
Jadams1!	
Password	
P@ssw0rd	

11. Once you successfully set the password, the *Make Changes To JAdam's Account* page re-appears.

12. Click Manage Another Account. The Choose The User Account You Would Like To Change window appears.

13. Take a screen shot of the Choose The User Account You Would Like To Change window with the new account you created by pressing Ctrl+Prt Scr, and then paste the resulting image into the lab05_worksheet file in the page provided by pressing Ctrl+V.

14. Close the User Accounts Control Panel.

15. Leave the computer logged on for the next exercise.

Exercise 5.3	Using the Local Users And Groups Snap-in
Overview	You have discovered that while the User Accounts screen makes it easy to create accounts for local users, it does not provide access to all of the user account properties you need to secure the computer. Therefore, you decide to create the rest of the local accounts for the computer using the Local Users And Groups snap-in for Microsoft Management Console (MMC) instead.
Completion time	20 minutes

1. Click Start, and then click Control Panel > System And Maintenance > Administrative Tools. The Administrative Tools window appears.

2. Double-click Computer Management. After confirming that you performed the action, the Computer Management console appears.

3. Expand the Local Users And Groups folder, and select the Users subfolder. A list of user accounts on the computer appears in the details pane.

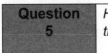

Question 5	How does the list of users in the snap-in differ from the list in the User Accounts control panel?

4. Double-click the JAdams user account. The JAdams Properties dialog box appears.

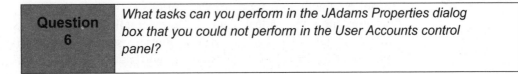

Question 6	What tasks can you perform in the JAdams Properties dialog box that you could not perform in the User Accounts control panel?

5. In the Full Name text box, key **Jay Adams**. Make sure the Password Never Expires checkbox is clear. Select the User Must Change Password At Next Logon checkbox and then click OK.

6. Right-click the Users folder and, from the context menu, select New User. The New User dialog box appears.

7. Create the user accounts listed in Table 5-4 and include the specified properties.

Table 5-4
New local user information

Full Name	Account Name	Password	Position	Selected Checkboxes
Pilar Ackerman	PAckerman	P@ssw0rd	Bookkeeper (Day)	User Must Change Password At Next Logon
Adam Barr	ABarr	P@ssw0rd	Shift Supervisor (Day)	User Must Change Password At Next Logon
Susan Metters	SMetters	P@ssw0rd	Bookkeeper (Night)	User Must Change Password At Next Logon
Heidi Steen	HSteen	P@ssw0rd	Shift Supervisor (Night)	User Must Change Password At Next Logon
Tai Yee	TYee	P@ssw0rd	Administrative Assistant	User Must Change Password At Next Logon

8. Take a screen shot of the Computer Management console with the new accounts you created by pressing Ctrl+Prt Scr, and then paste the resulting image into the lab05_worksheet file in the page provided by pressing Ctrl+V.

9. Leave the Computer Management console open for the next exercise.

Exercise 5.4	Managing Group Memberships
Overview	When you create local user accounts with the User Accounts control panel, you have two account type options (Standard User and Administrator) to choose from that are actually a means of creating memberships in the Users and Administrators groups, respectively. In the Local Users And Groups snap-in, you must manually configure the group memberships for the new users.
	The IT director of Contoso, Ltd. has ordered that every workgroup computer have two additional local groups created on it, called Accounting and Bookkeeping. He has also provided you with the following group membership assignments that must be implemented on every workgroup computer.
	• Accounting – Director, shift supervisors, administrative assistants
	• Bookkeeping – Director, bookkeepers, administrative assistants
	• Administrators – Director, shift supervisors
	• Power Users – Director, bookkeepers
	• Users – Director, shift supervisors, bookkeepers, administrative assistants
Completion time	20 minutes

1. In the Computer Management console, click the Groups folder.

> **Question 7**
>
> *How many built-in groups can be found on the computer?*

2. Right-click the Groups folder and, from the context menu, select New Group. The New Group dialog box appears.

3. In the Group Name text box, key **Accounting** and click Create. After creating the group, the dialog box resets itself.

4. In the Group Name text box, key **Bookkeeping**. Click Create, and then click Close.

5. In the Users folder, open the Properties dialog box for the JAdams account you created in Exercise 5.2 and click the Member Of tab.

> **Question 8**
>
> *Of which group(s) is Jay Adams currently a member?*

6. Click Add. The Select Groups dialog box appears.

7. In the Enter The Object Names To Select text box, key **Accounting; Bookkeeping; Administrators; Power Users**. Click Check Names, and then click OK. The groups appear in the Member Of list.

8. Click OK to close the JAdams Properties dialog box.

9. Using the account information in Table 5-4 and the membership assignments at the beginning of this exercise, create the appropriate group memberships for all of the users you created in Exercise 5.3.

10. Leave the Computer Management console open for the next exercise.

Exercise 5.5	Configuring Logon Behavior
Overview	Now that you have created the new local user accounts and group memberships on the workstation, you will perform tests to make sure that the accounts are functioning as intended and the computer is adequately secured.
Completion time	20 minutes

1. In the Computer Management console, open the JAdams Properties dialog box. Then, clear the User Must Change Password At Next Logon checkbox and click OK.

2. Close all open windows and log off.

3. Log on using the JAdams user account and the password you specified in Exercise 5.2.

4. Open the Local Security Policy console as you did in Exercise 5.1.

5. Expand the Local Policies Node and select Security Options. A list of security options appears in the details pane.

6. Scroll down the list and double-click the Interactive Logon: Do Not Display Last User Name policy. The Interactive Logon: Do Not Display Last User Name Properties dialog box appears.

7. Click the Enabled radio button and click OK.

8. Double-click the Interactive Logon: Do Not Require CTRL+ALT+DEL policy. The Interactive Logon: Do Not Require CTRL+ALT+DEL Properties dialog box appears.

9. Click the Disabled radio button and click OK.

10. Close the Local Security Policy console and log off.

11. Log on again using the JAdams account.

Question 9	How idoes the method by which you logged on differ as a result of the security policy changes you just made?

12. Open the Computer Management console. In the JAdams Properties dialog box, re-enable the User Must Change Password At Next Logon checkbox, and then click OK.

13. Close all console windows and log off.

LAB REVIEW QUESTIONS

Completion time	10 minutes

1. In Exercise 5.1, does increasing the Minimum Password Age value from 0 to 6 decrease or increase the security of the network? Explain why.

2. How is the default method for logging on to a Windows Vista workgroup computer inherently insecure?

3. How is the logon method you used at the end of Exercise 5.5 more secure than the default Windows Vista workgroup logon method?

4. Assume that the Account Lockout policies for your domain are set to the values shown in the following table. What changes could you make to the policy values that would increase the security of the network? Explain your answer.

Account Lockout Policy	Value
Account lockout duration	0
Account lockout threshold	3 invalid logon attempts
Reset Account Lockout After	5 minutes

5. In Exercise 5.1, would reducing the value of the Enforce Password History policy increase or decrease the security of the network? Explain your answer.

LAB CHALLENGE: USING NET.EXE

Completion time	25 minutes

In addition to its graphical user management tools, Windows Vista also enables you to create and manage users and groups from the command line by using the Net.exe utility. With Net.exe, you can create batch files that automate user management tasks. To complete this challenge, write a batch file that creates the users, groups, and group memberships shown in Table 5-5. To create account names for the users, add the first initial to the surname, and assign each user the password **P@ssw0rd**.

Table 5-5

Sales	OrderEntry	QualityControl
Zainal Arifin	John Fredericksen	Craig Playstead
Randall Boseman	Kevin Wright	Kevin Wright
Keith Harris	Eric Rothenberg	David Campbell
Jeff Dulong	Randall Boseman	Misty Shock
Misty Shock	Cathan Cook	Randall Boseman

LAB 6
WORKING WITH PRINTERS

This lab contains the following exercises and activities:

Exercise 6.1   Installing a Printer

Exercise 6.2   Sharing a Printer

Exercise 6.3   Controlling Access to a Printer

Exercise 6.4   Creating an Additional Logical Printer

Lab Review   Questions

Lab Challenge   Creating a Printer Pool

BEFORE YOU BEGIN

Lab 6 assumes that setup has been completed as specified in the setup document, that your workstation has connectivity to the classroom network and other lab computers, and that you have completed the exercises in Labs 1 through 5. At this point, there should be two copies of Windows Vista installed on the student workstation, one clean installation that you performed in Lab 1 and one upgrade that you performed in Lab 3.

Before you start this lab, make sure you have the following information for your workstation:

Student workstation name (Computer##)	
Student account name (Student##)	

Working with Lab Worksheets

Each lab in this manual requires that you answer questions, shoot screen shots, or perform other activities that you will document in a worksheet named for the lab, such as lab01_worksheet.doc. You will find these worksheets on your student CD. As you perform the exercises in each lab, open the appropriate worksheet file using WordPad, fill in the required information, and save the file to your student folder on the SERVER01 computer. Your instructor will examine these worksheet files to assess your performance. At the end of each lab, make sure that you save your fully completed worksheet file to the server and not to your local drive.

The procedure for opening and saving a worksheet file is as follows:

1. Click Start, and then click Run. The Run dialog box appears.

2. In the Open text box, browse your student CD to find the worksheet for this lab. Click Open and then click OK.

3. The worksheet document opens in WordPad.

4. Complete all exercises in the worksheet.

5. In WordPad, choose Save As from the File menu. The Save As dialog box appears.

6. In the File Name text box, key
    \\server01\students\student##\lab##_worksheet_*yourname* (where student## contains your student number, lab## contains the number of the lab you're working on, and *yourname* is your last name).

SCENARIO

You are a Windows Vista desktop support technician for Contoso, Ltd., a company with workstations in a variety of different environments. You have been assigned the task of installing and managing a number of new printers that the company has just received.

After completing this lab, you will be able to:

- Install and share a printer

- Install additional printer drivers

- Configure advanced printer properties

- Configure printer permissions

Estimated lab time: 115 minutes

Exercise 6.1	Installing a Printer
Overview	Contoso, Ltd. has just taken delivery of several new printers that the IT director purchased through an auction. He has assigned you the task of installing the printers and making them available to the users of the company network. For the first printer, you intend to connect the unit directly to an LPT port in the computer that will function as the print server. In this exercise, you install the driver for the printer and configure it to send print jobs to the LPT2 port.
Completion time	20 minutes

1. Turn on your workstation and, when the boot menu appears, select the clean copy of Windows Vista that you installed in Lab 1.

2. Log on to the local machine using the student## account.

3. Open the Run dialog box and browse your student CD to find the worksheet for this lab. Click Open and then click OK. The worksheet document opens in WordPad.

4. In WordPad, choose File > Save As. The Save As dialog box appears.

5. Save a copy of the file to the \\server01\students\student## folder.

6. When prompted, log on to server01 using the student## account and the password **P@ssw0rd**.

7. Leave the lab06_worksheet file open in WordPad and answer the questions in the document as they appear in the lab. If you must restart the computer, be sure to reopen the copy of the worksheet on the Server01 server.

8. Click Start, and then click Control Panel > Hardware And Sound > Printers. The Printers window appears.

9. Click Add A Printer. The *Choose A Local Or Network Printer* page appears.

10. Click Add A Local Printer. The *Choose A Printer Port* page appears.

11. With the Use An Existing Port radio button selected, select LPT2: (Printer Port) from the drop-down list and click Next. The *Install The Printer Driver* page appears.

Question 1	Why doesn't Windows Vista attempt to automatically detect a printer connected to the computer?

12. In the Manufacturers column, select HP. In the Printers column, select HP LaserJet 5200 Series PCL 5 and click Next. The *Type A Printer Name* page appears.

13. In the Printer Name text box, key **HPLJ5200** and click Next. The *You've Successfully Added HPLJ5200* page appears.

14. Click Finish. The HPLJ5200 icon appears in the Printers window.

15. Take a screen shot of the Printers window with the new printer icon you created by pressing Alt+Prt Scr, and then paste the resulting image into the lab06_worksheet file in the page provided by pressing Ctrl+V.

16. Leave the Printers window open for the next exercise.

Exercise 6.2	Sharing a Printer
Overview	With the printer installed on the computer, you are ready to make it available to network users by creating a printer share and publishing it in the Active Directory database.
Completion time	20 minutes

1. In the Printers window, right-click the HPLJ5200 printer icon you created in Exercise 6.1 and, from the context menu, select Properties. The HPLJ5200 Properties sheet appears.

2. Click the Sharing tab, and then click Change Sharing Options. The Sharing tab appears with most of its controls deactivated.

3. After confirming your action, the Sharing tab appears with its controls activated as shown in Figure 6-1.

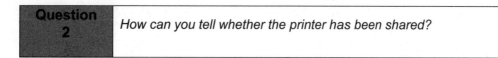

Figure 6-1
The Sharing tab of a printer's Properties sheet

4. Select the Share This Printer checkbox. Leave the Render Print Jobs On Client Computers checkbox selected, and then click OK.

Question 2	How can you tell whether the printer has been shared?

5. Leave the Printers window open for the next exercise.

Exercise 6.3	Controlling Access to a Printer
Overview	The new printer you installed has been in use for several weeks, and there have been some administrative problems you must address. First, from reading the printer's page counter and the amount of paper consumed, it is apparent that someone is using the printer to generate an enormous amount of personal work after business hours. While it is not practical to secure the printer physically, you can restrict the hours in which it can be used. In addition, you can limit who has access to the printer by using permissions. Another problem is that users are sending print jobs requiring paper of various sizes to the printer, and when a specific type of paper is not available, the entire print queue is halted until someone inserts the correct paper for that particular job. There have also been several instances in which a user's computer crashed while printing a job and in which a user tried to interrupt a job as it was printing, thereby causing the queue to be stalled until the partial job was removed. In this exercise, you configure the advanced properties of the logical printer you created in Exercise 6.1 to create a more secure printing environment and prevent these problems from occurring.
Completion time	20 minutes

1. Open the HPLJ5200 Properties sheet and click the Advanced tab as shown in Figure 6-2.

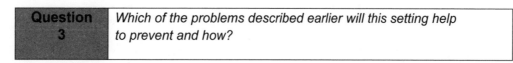

Figure 6-2
The Advanced tab of a printer's Properties sheet

2. Select the Available From radio button and, in the two spin boxes provided, set the time that the printer is available to 9:00 AM to 5:00 PM.

Question 3	Which of the problems described earlier will this setting help to prevent and how?

3. Select the Start Printing After Last Page Is Spooled radio button.

4. Select the Hold Mismatched Documents checkbox.

5. Click Apply, and then click the Security tab as shown in Figure 6-3.

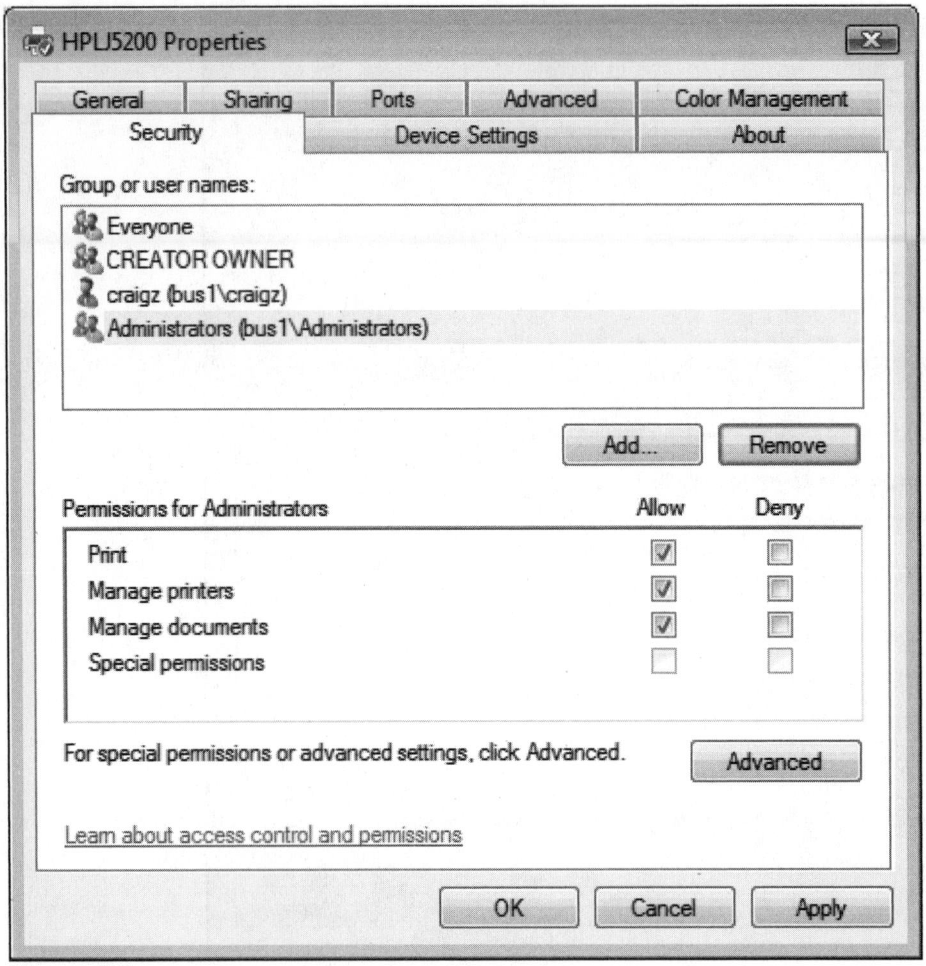

Figure 6-3
The Security tab of a printer's Properties sheet

6. In the Group Or User Names list, select Everyone and click Remove. The Everyone special identity is removed from the Group Or User Names list.

7. Click Add. The Select Users Or Groups dialog box appears.

8. In the Enter The Object Names To Select box, key **Users** and click OK. The Users security principal appears in the Group Or User Names list.

9. With Users highlighted, make sure that only the Print checkbox in the Allow column is selected.

10. Make sure that the Administrators group is listed as a security principal and is assigned the Print, Manage Printers, and Manage Documents permissions in the Allow column.

11. Take a screen shot of the Security tab with the new permissions you created by pressing Alt+Prt Scr, and then paste the resulting image into the lab06_worksheet file in the page provided by pressing Ctrl+V.

12. Click OK to close the Properties sheet.

13. Leave the Printers window open for the next exercise.

Exercise 6.4	Creating an Additional Logical Printer
Overview	After modifying the printer permissions and other properties in Exercise 6.3, you have found that the unauthorized use of the HPLJ5200 printer has stopped. However, you received some complaints from company executives who wanted to use the printer during a late meeting with clients and were unable to do so because it was past 5:00 PM. Some of these executives were also upset because their print jobs had to wait in the queue, just like everyone else's. As a result, you must find a way to provide selected users with unlimited, priority printer access, while still limiting the access granted to other users.
	In this exercise, you create a second printer for the same print device and use it to provide additional access to the late-working executives (whom you have added to the Administrators group on the print server computer).
Completion time	20 minutes

1. In the Printers window, create a new printer for the HP LaserJet 5200 printer connected to the computer's LPT2 port. Give the local printer the name HPLJ5200-2.

2. Share the HPLJ5200-2 printer using the share name HPLJ5200-2, configuring the Sharing tab by using the same settings you applied in Exercise 6.2.

3. Open the HPLJ5200-2 Properties sheet and click the Advanced tab.

4. Make sure the Always Available option is selected, and change the value of the Priority spin box from 1 to 99.

Question 4	How will modifying the Priority value help to achieve the goals stated at the beginning of this exercise?

5. Click Apply, and then click the Security tab.

6. In the Group Or User Names list, remove the Everyone security principal.

7. Make sure that the Administrators group is listed as a security principal and is assigned the Print, Manage Printers, and Manage Documents permissions in the Allow column.

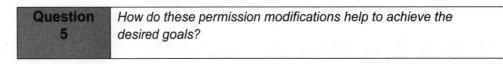

Question 5	How do these permission modifications help to achieve the desired goals?

8. Close the HPLJ5200-2 Properties dialog box.

9. Log off of the computer.

LAB REVIEW QUESTIONS

Completion time   10 minutes

1. Does leaving the Print Jobs On Client Computers checkbox selected increase or decrease the processor burden on the computer hosting the printer?

2. In Exercise 6.3, which of the problems described at the beginning of the exercise will selecting the Start Printing After Last Page Is Spooled radio button help to prevent, and how?

3. In Exercise 6.3, which of the problems described at the beginning of the exercise will selecting the Hold Mismatched Documents checkbox help to prevent, and how?

4. In Exercise 6.3, how do the changes in the permission assignments you made enhance the security of the printer installation?

LAB CHALLENGE: CREATING A PRINTER POOL

Completion time	25 minutes

As the next phase of the printer deployment at Contoso, Ltd., the IT director has allocated five identical LaserJet 5200 printers to be used as a printer pool for the Order Entry department. Unlike the HPLJ5200 printer you installed earlier in this lab, which connected to the computer using an LPT port, these five printers all have Hewlett Packard JetDirect network interface adapters in them that have already been assigned the following IP addresses:

- 10.1.5.2
- 10.1.5.3
- 10.1.5.4
- 10.1.5.5
- 10.1.5.6

To complete this challenge, your task is to create a printer on your workstation and share it with the network using the name HPLJ5200 OE Pool. You then configure the printer to function as a printer pool using the IP addresses cited earlier. Write out the procedure you used to create and configure the printer, and then take a screen shot [ALT+PRT SCR] of the Ports tab in the HPLJ5200 OE Pool Properties sheet and paste it into your worksheet.

LAB 7
NETWORKING WITH WINDOWS VISTA

This lab contains the following exercises and activities:

Exercise 7.1   Using the Network And Sharing Center

Exercise 7.2   Using Network Map

Exercise 7.3   Manually Configuring TCP/IP

Exercise 7.4   Testing Network Connections

Lab Review   Questions

Lab Challenge   Configuring Multiple IP Addresses

BEFORE YOU BEGIN

Lab 7 assumes that setup has been completed as specified in the setup document, that your workstation has connectivity to the classroom network and other lab computers, and that you have completed the exercises in Labs 1 to 6. At this point, there should be two copies of Windows Vista installed on the student workstation, one clean installation that you performed in Lab 1 and one upgrade that you performed in Lab 3.

Before you start this lab, make sure you have the following information for your workstation:

Student workstation name (Computer##)	
Student account name (Student##)	

Working with Lab Worksheets

Each lab in this manual requires that you answer questions, shoot screen shots, or perform other activities that you will document in a worksheet named for the lab, such as lab01_worksheet.doc. You will find these worksheets on your student CD. As you perform the exercises in each lab, open the appropriate worksheet file using WordPad, fill in the required information, and save the file to your student folder on the SERVER01 computer. Your instructor will examine these worksheet files to assess your performance. At the end of each lab, make sure that you save your fully completed worksheet file to the server and not to your local drive.

The procedure for opening and saving a worksheet file is as follows:

1. Click Start, and then click Run. The Run dialog box appears.

2. In the Open text box, browse your student CD to find the worksheet for this lab. Click Open and then click OK.

3. The worksheet document opens in WordPad.

4. Complete all exercises in the worksheet.

5. In WordPad, choose Save As from the File menu. The Save As dialog box appears.

6. In the File Name text box, key
   \\server01\students\student##\lab##_worksheet_*yourname* (where student## contains your student number, lab## contains the number of the lab you're working on, and *yourname* is your last name).

SCENARIO

You are a Windows Vista desktop support technician for Contoso, Ltd., a company with workstations in a variety of different environments. The IT director wants to create a permanent software testing lab where engineers can run updates and new applications prior to deploying them on the network. The lab will consist of a network that can function in complete isolation from the company's production network. You have been assigned the task of building the lab network using Windows Vista computers borrowed from the production network.

After completing this lab, you will be able to:

- Use the Windows Vista Network And Sharing Center

- Use Network Map

■ Manually configure the Windows Vista TCP/IP client

■ Test network connections with Ping

Estimated lab time: 90 minutes

Exercise 7.1	Using the Network And Sharing Center
Overview	On a Windows Vista computer, the Network And Sharing Center provides access to most of the operating system's networking tools and configuration parameters. In this exercise, you examine the current Sharing And Discovery settings on one of the computers that will become part of the lab network and determine how the network type affects those settings.
Completion time	20 minutes

1. Turn on your workstation and, when the boot menu appears, select the clean copy of Windows Vista you installed in Lab 3.

2. Log on to the local machine using the student## account.

3. Open the Run dialog box and browse your student CD to find the worksheet for this lab. Click Open and then click OK. The worksheet document opens in WordPad.

4. In WordPad, choose File > Save As. The Save As dialog box appears.

5. Save a copy of the file to the \\server01\students\student## folder.

6. When prompted, log on to Server01 using the student## account and the password **P@ssw0rd**.

7. Leave the lab07_worksheet file open in WordPad and answer the questions in the document as they appear in the lab. If you must restart the computer, be sure to reopen the copy of the worksheet on the Server01 server.

8. Click Start, and then click Control Panel > Network And Internet > Network And Sharing Center. The Network And Sharing Center window appears as shown in Figure 7-1.

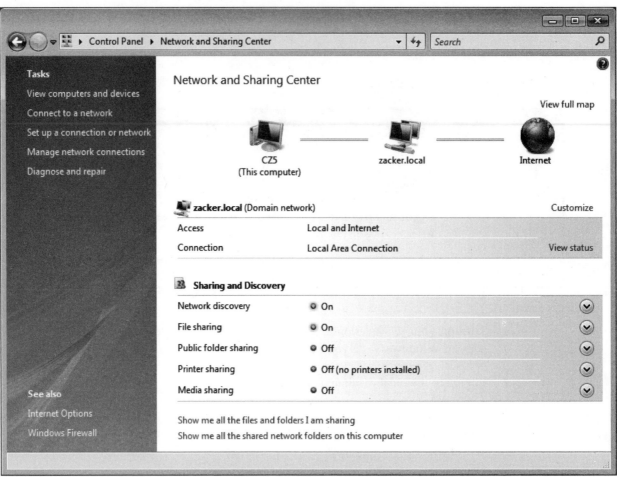

Figure 7-1
The Network And Sharing Center

9. In Table 7-1, note the current state of the Sharing And Discovery settings.

Table 7-1

Sharing And Discovery Settings	
Network Discovery	On
File Sharing	On
Public Folder Sharing	Off
Printer Sharing	Off
Password Protected Sharing	On
Media Sharing	Off

10. Click the Customize button. The Set Network Location Wizard launches, and the *Customize Network Settings* page appears. Select the Public radio button and click Next.

11. After confirming that you performed the action, the *Successfully Set Network Settings* page appears. Click Close.

Question 1	What changes are evident on the Network And Sharing Center page as a result of the change from a private to a public network? How will these changes affect the functionality of the computer?

12. Leave the Network And Sharing Center open for the next exercise.

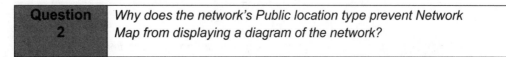

Exercise 7.2	Using Network Map
Overview	In this exercise, you use Network Map to diagram the network, so you plan the software deployments for the lab network at a later time.
Completion time	10 minutes

1. In the Network And Sharing Center window, click View Full Map. The *Network Map* page appears.

Question 2	Why does the network's Public location type prevent Network Map from displaying a diagram of the network?

2. Open the Set Network Location Wizard (as you did in Exercise 7.1), and set the network location type to Private.

3. Switch to the Network And Sharing Center and click View Full Map again. The Network Map window appears, displaying a diagram of the network.

4. Take a screen shot of the Network Map window by pressing Alt+Prt Scr, and then paste the resulting image into the lab07_worksheet file in the page provided by pressing Ctrl+V.

5. Close all windows and log off of the computer.

Exercise 7.3	Manually Configuring TCP/IP
Overview	Because the lab network you are constructing for Contoso, Ltd. must be isolated from the production network, you do not want the lab computers to obtain their TCP/IP settings from the DHCP servers on the production network. Therefore, you must configure the TCP/IP client to use static IP addresses.
Completion time	20 minutes

1. Click Start, point to All Programs, point to Accessories, and click Command Prompt. A Command Prompt window appears.

2. In the Command Prompt window, key **ipconfig /all** and press Enter.

3. Using the information in the Ipconfig display, note your workstation's current TCP/IP configuration settings in Table 7-2.

Table 7-2

TCP/IP Setting	Value
IPv4 Address	
Subnet Mask	
Default Gateway	
DNS Servers	

Question 3	How did the computer obtain these settings? How can you determine this?

4. In the Command Prompt window, key **ipconfig /release** and press Enter.

Question 4	What is the result of this command?

5. In the Network And Sharing Center window, click Manage Network Connections. The Network Connections window appears.

6. Right-click the Local Area Connection icon and, from the context menu, select Properties. After confirming your action, the Local Area Connection Properties sheet appears.

7. Select Internet Protocol Version 4 (TCP/IPv4) from the components list and click Properties. The Internet Protocol Version 4 (TCP/IPv4) Properties sheet appears as shown in Figure 7-2.

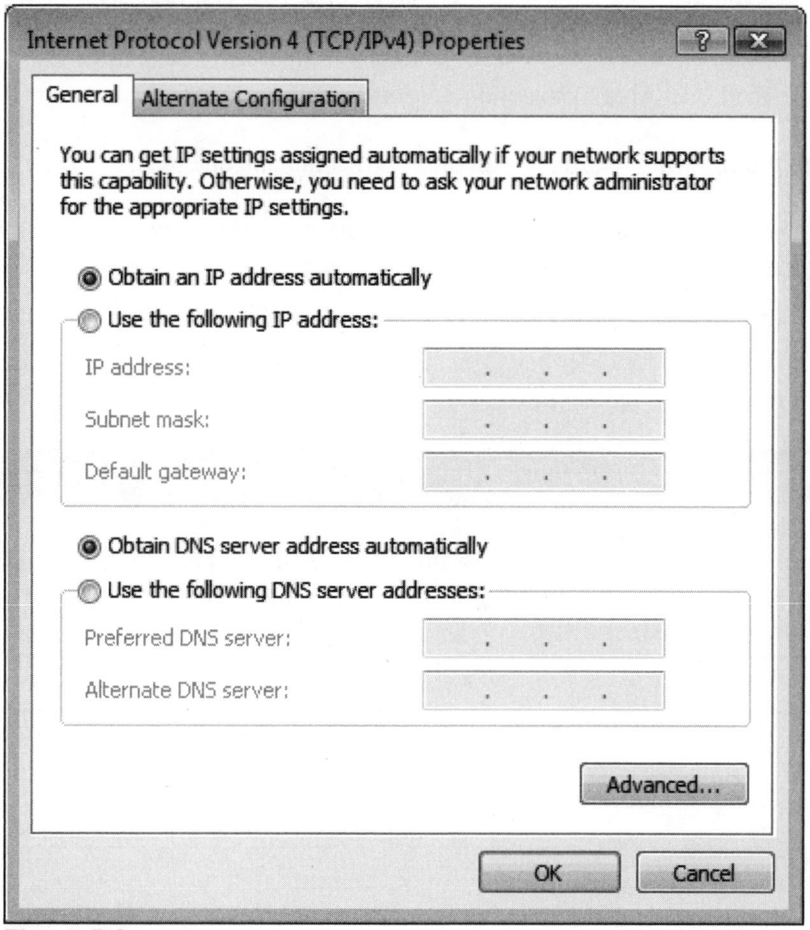

Figure 7-2
The Internet Protocol Version 4 (TCP/IPv4) Properties sheet

8. Select the Use The Following IP Address radio button.

9. In the IP Address text box, key the IPv4 Address value from Table 7-2, changing the network address from 10.1.1.x to 10.2.1.x.

10. In the Subnet Mask text box, key the Subnet Mask value from the table.

11. In the Default Gateway text box, key the Default Gateway value from the table.

12. In the Preferred DNS Server text box, key the DNS Server value from the table.

13. Take a screen shot of the Internet Protocol Version 4 (TCP/IPv4) Properties sheet by pressing Alt+Prt Scr, and then paste the resulting image into the lab07_worksheet file in the page provided by pressing Ctrl+V.

14. Click OK to close the Internet Protocol Version 4 (TCP/IPv4) Properties sheet.

15. Click OK to close the Local Area Connection Properties sheet.

16. In the Command Prompt window, run the **ipconfig /all** command again.

Question 5	How does the Ipconfig display differ from the first time you ran the ipconfig /all command?

17. Leave the windows open for the next exercise.

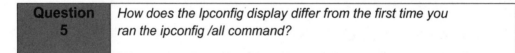

Exercise 7.4	Testing Network Connections
Overview	After manually configuring the Windows Vista TCP/IP client, you must test it by trying to connect to the other computers on the network. In this exercise, you use the Ping utility to test the computer's communications capabilities.
Completion time	20 minutes

1. In the Command Prompt window, key **ping 127.0.0.1** and press Enter.

Question 6	What is the result?
Question 7	What does this result prove about the computer's network connectivity?

2. In the Command Prompt window, key **ping server01** and press Enter.

Question 8	What is the result of the ping test, and what does it prove?
Question 9	What is Server01's IP address?
Question 10	How was the computer able to resolve the name Server01 into its IP address?

3. Ask another student to provide you with the IP address of his or her computer, and test your connectivity to it using the command **ping ipaddress**.

Question 11	What was the result of the test, and what does this result prove?

4. Ask the other student to ping your computer by using the IP address you assigned to it.

Question 12	What was the result of the test, and what does this result prove?
Question 13	Was it necessary to perform this last test? Why or why not?

LAB REVIEW QUESTIONS

Completion time	10 minutes

1. In Exercise 7.1, which of the parameters in the Internet Protocol Version 4 (TCP/IPv4) Properties sheet would you have to omit for your computer to be unable to resolve the Server01 name into its IP address?

2. In Exercise 7.3, what would be the result if you unplugged your computer's network cable before executing the ping 127.0.0.1 command?

3. In Exercise 7.4, why are you unable to see the other computers on the network in the Explorer window when you were able to ping them earlier?

4. In Exercise 7.2, why does the Server01 computer not appear on the Network Map display?

LAB CHALLENGE: CONFIGURING MULTIPLE IP ADDRESSES

Completion time	10 minutes

To separate the new lab network's TCP/IP traffic from that of the production network, you must assign IP addresses to the lab computers on a different network. To complete this challenge, configure the TCP/IP client on your computer to use a second IP address in addition to the one you configured earlier in this lab. For the second IP address, use 10.3.1.##, where ## is the number of your computer. Take a screen shot of the dialog box containing the two IP addresses by pressing Alt+Prt Scr, and then paste the resulting image into the lab07_worksheet file in the page provided by pressing Ctrl+V.

LAB 8
SHARING FILES AND FOLDERS

This lab contains the following exercises and activities:

Exercise 8.1   Configuring Folder Options

Exercise 8.2   Configuring File Associations

Exercise 8.3   Compressing Files and Folders

Exercise 8.4   Creating Shares

Exercise 8.5   Working with NTFS Permissions

Lab Review   Questions

Lab Challenge   Encrypting Files and Folders

BEFORE YOU BEGIN

Lab 8 assumes that setup has been completed as specified in the setup document, that your workstation has connectivity to the classroom network and other lab computers, and that you have completed the exercises in Labs 1 to 7. At this point, there should be two copies of Windows Vista installed on the student workstation, one clean installation that you performed in Lab 1 and one upgrade that you performed in Lab 3.

Before you start this lab, make sure you have the following information for your workstation:

Student workstation name (Computer##)	
Student account name (Student##)	

Working with Lab Worksheets

Each lab in this manual requires that you answer questions, shoot screen shots, or perform other activities that you will document in a worksheet named for the lab, such as lab01_worksheet.doc. You will find these worksheets on your student CD. As you perform the exercises in each lab, open the appropriate worksheet file using WordPad, fill in the required information, and save the file to your student folder on the SERVER01 computer. Your instructor will examine these worksheet files to assess your performance. At the end of each lab, make sure that you save your fully completed worksheet file to the server and not to your local drive.

The procedure for opening and saving a worksheet file is as follows:

1. Click Start, and then click Run. The Run dialog box appears.

2. In the Open text box, browse your student CD to find the worksheet for this lab. Click Open and then click OK.

3. The worksheet document opens in WordPad.

4. Complete all exercises in the worksheet.

5. In WordPad, choose Save As from the File menu. The Save As dialog box appears.

6. In the File Name text box, key
   \\server01\students\student##\lab##_worksheet_*yourname* (where student## contains your student number, lab## contains the number of the lab you're working on, and *yourname* is your last name).

SCENARIO

You are a Windows Vista support technician for Contoso, Ltd., a company with workstations in a variety of different environments. You are currently assigned to the desktop support help desk and, as a result, you are faced with a number of problems concerning file sharing and access control.

After completing this lab, you will be able to:

- ■ Configure folder options and file associations

- ■ Compress files and folders

- ■ Create and control access to shares

- ■ Modify NTFS permissions

Estimated lab time: 135 minutes

Exercise 8.1	Configuring Folder Options
Overview	You are a desktop technician for Contoso, Ltd. who has been given the task of configuring several new Windows Vista computers for the network support staff. Because these users have more computing experience than most other company employees, you will be configuring the Windows interface to provide the users with greater access to the operating system than you would for other users. In this exercise, you modify the folder options on a computer to display file extensions and hidden files.
Completion time	20 minutes

1. Turn on your workstation and, when the boot menu appears, select the clean copy of Windows Vista you installed in Lab 3.

2. Click Start, and then click All Programs > Accessories > Windows Explorer. A Windows Explorer window appears.

3. Expand the Computer container and select the Local Disk (C:) icon.

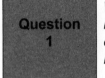 **Question 1**	*When a Windows Vista computer starts, it uses files in the root of the C: drive and the C:\Boot folder to load the operating system. Why can't you see the boot folder and files in Windows Explorer?*

4. On the C: drive, select the Windows folder.

5. From the Views drop-down list, select Details. Windows Explorer changes to a columnar display.

6. Locate a file in the C:\Windows folder called System.

Question 2	*What type of file is System? How can you determine this?*
Question 3	*Based only on the information in the Windows Explorer display, what is the file extension of the System file?*

7. Click Start, and then click Control Panel > Appearance And Personalization > Folder Options. The Folder Options dialog box appears.

8. On the General tab in the Tasks box, select the Use Windows Classic Folders radio button.

9. In the Browse Folders box, select the Open Each Folder In The Same Window radio button.

10. Click the View tab.

11. In the Advanced Settings list, make the following modifications, as shown in Figure 8-1:

    - Select the Display The Full Path In The Title Bar checkbox.
    - Select the Show Hidden Files And Folders option.
    - Clear the Hide Extensions For Known File Types checkbox.
    - Clear the Hide Protected Operating System Files checkbox, answering Yes when the Warning message box appears.
    - Clear the Remember Each Folder's View Settings checkbox.

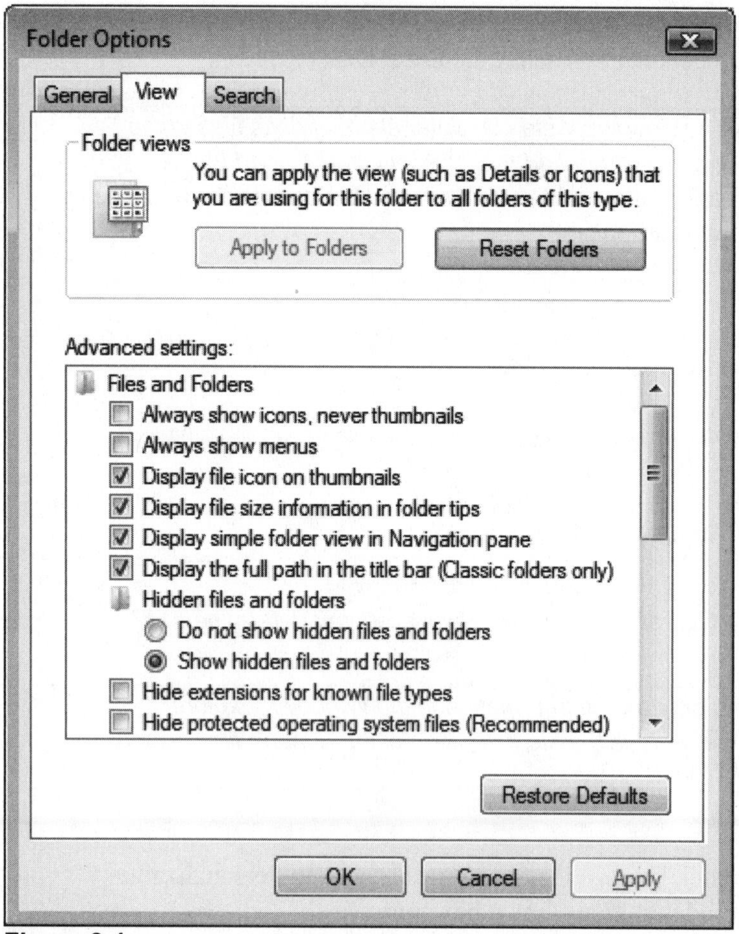

Figure 8-1
The View tab in the Folder Options dialog box

12. Click OK.

13. Return to the Windows Explorer window and click the Local Disk (C:) icon.

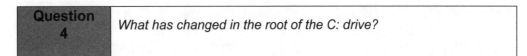

Question 4	*What has changed in the root of the C: drive?*

14. Take a screen shot of the Windows Explorer window showing the root of the C: drive by pressing Alt+Prt Scr, and then paste the resulting image into the lab08_worksheet file in the page provided by pressing Ctrl+V.

15. Click the Windows folder and locate the System file you looked at earlier.

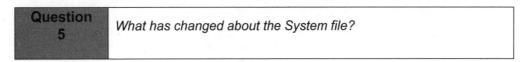

Question 5	*What has changed about the System file?*

16. Leave the Windows Explorer window open for the next exercise.

Exercise 8.2	Configuring File Associations
Overview	Jinghao, an employee at Contoso, Ltd., has been given a large number of JPEG graphic files by her supervisor, who has instructed her to resize each file, rotate it 90 degrees, and print it. She plans to use the Windows Vista Paint application for this task, but has found that Windows Vista opens JPEG files in the Windows Photo Gallery application by default. Jinghao calls the desktop support help desk where you are working and asks whether you could fix her computer so that she can double-click a JPEG file and have it open in Paint. In this exercise, you modify the file association for JPEG files on Jinghao's computer.
Completion time	20 minutes

1. In Windows Explorer, browse to the C:\Users\Public\Public Pictures\Sample Pictures folder and double-click one of the image files there.

Question 6	*What happens?*

2. Click Start, and then click Control Panel > Programs > Default Programs. The *Choose The Programs That Windows Uses By Default* page appears.

3. Click Associate A File Type Or Protocol With A Program. The Associate A File Type Or Protocol With A Specific Program dialog box appears as shown in Figure 8-2.

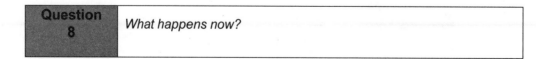

Figure 8-2
The Associate A File Type Or Protocol With A Specific Program dialog box

4. Scroll down the list of extensions and locate the .jpg extension.

Question 7	What application is currently associated with the .jpg extension?

5. Select the entry for the .jpg extension and click Change Program. The Open With dialog box appears.

6. Select the Paint application, click OK, and then click Close.

7. Double-click the image file you selected earlier.

Question 8	What happens now?

8. Leave the windows open for the next exercise.

Exercise 8.3	Compressing Files and Folders
Overview	A user named Calvin calls the desktop support help desk where you are working. He tells you that he must copy a number of large image files to his local drive, but an error has appeared on his computer stating that he does not have enough disk space. Calvin claims that he needs all of the files on his hard disk and that there is nothing he can delete to make room for the new files. You decide to compress some of the files on Calvin's drive to provide him with more space. In this exercise, you create a compressed folder and demonstrate the effects of copying and moving files to and from that folder.
Completion time	20 minutes

1. Open Internet Explorer, key **\\Server01** in the address box, and press Enter. An Internet Explorer Security message box appears.

2. Click Allow. A Network Explorer window appears, displaying the shares on Server01.

3. Double-click the VistaInstall share, and copy the Support folder to the root of the C: drive on your computer.

4. Right-click the C:\Support folder you just created on your computer and, from the context menu, select Properties. The Support Properties sheet appears.

Question 9	*How many files and folders are in the Support folder?*
Question 10	*What is the Size value for the Support folder?*
Question 11	*What is the Size On Disk value of the Documents folder?*

5. Click Advanced. The Advanced Attributes dialog box appears as shown in Figure 8-3.

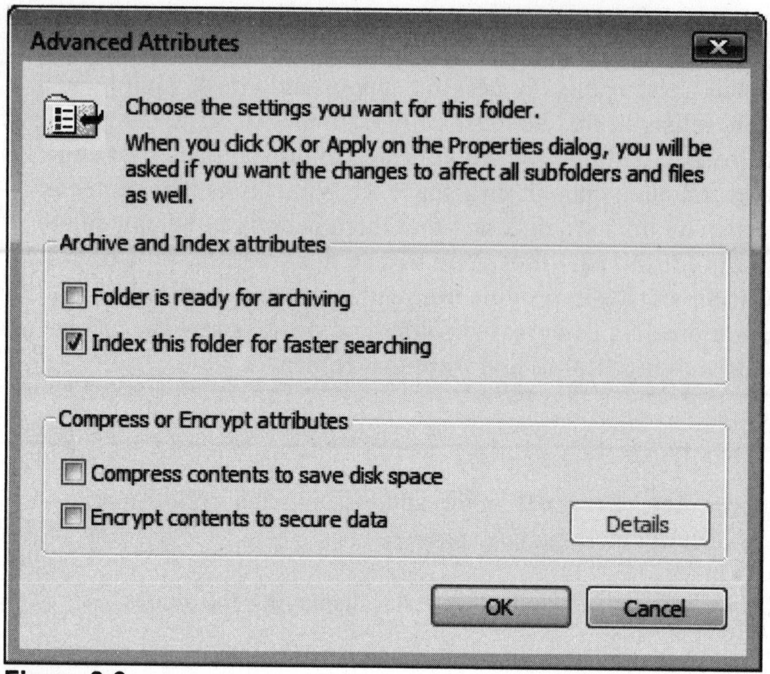

Advanced Attributes ☒

Choose the settings you want for this folder.

When you click OK or Apply on the Properties dialog, you will be asked if you want the changes to affect all subfolders and files as well.

Archive and Index attributes

☐ Folder is ready for archiving

☑ Index this folder for faster searching

Compress or Encrypt attributes

☐ Compress contents to save disk space

☐ Encrypt contents to secure data   Details

OK   Cancel

Figure 8-3
The Advanced Attributes dialog box

6. In the Compress Or Encrypt Attributes box, select the Compress Contents To Save Disk Space checkbox, and then click OK.

7. Click OK again to close the Documents Properties dialog box. The Confirm Attribute Changes dialog box appears, prompting you to confirm whether you want to compress only the Documents folder or its subfolders and files as well.

8. Click OK to accept the default Apply Changes To This Folder, Subfolders, And Files value.

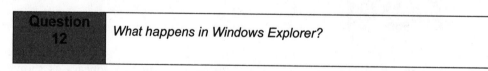

Question 12	What happens in Windows Explorer?

9. Open the Support Properties sheet again.

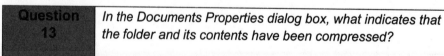

Question 13	In the Documents Properties dialog box, what indicates that the folder and its contents have been compressed?

10. Take a screen shot of the Support Properties sheet by pressing Alt+Prt Scr, and then paste the resulting image into the lab08_worksheet file in the page provided by pressing Ctrl+V.

11. Click OK to close the Support Properties sheet.

12. In the Support\Migwiz folder, select one of the compressed files and move it to the C:Users\student##\Documents folder, where ## is the number of the account you used to log on.

NOTE	Be sure to move the file. Do not copy it.
Question 14	Is the file still compressed? How can you determine this?

13. Select another file from the Support\Migwiz folder, and this time copy it to the C:Users\student## folder.

NOTE	Be sure to copy the file. Do not move it.
Question 15	Is the copy compressed?

14. On the root of the C: drive, select the Bootmgr file and copy it to the Support folder.

NOTE	Be sure to copy the Ntdetect.com file. Do not move it.
Question 16	Is the copy of the Bootmgr file compressed?

15. Leave the windows open for the next exercise.

Exercise 8.4	Creating Shares
Overview	Meena, a user with a Windows Vista workstation, has files on her local drive that she must share with other users on the network. However, these files must not be fully accessible to everyone. As the desktop support technician responding to Meena's request, you decide to create a standard share on the computer and use share permissions to control access to the files.
Completion time	20 minutes

1. In Windows Explorer, right-click the Support folder you created in Exercise 8.3. On the context menu, select Sharing And Security. The Support Properties sheet appears, with the Sharing tab selected.

2. Click Advanced Sharing. After you confirm the action, the Advanced Sharing dialog box appears.

3. Select the Share This Folder checkbox. The Support default value appears in the Share Name text box.

4. Click Permissions. The Permissions For Support dialog box appears.

5. For the Everyone special identity, clear all checkboxes in the Allow column.

6. Click Add. The Select Users Or Groups dialog box appears.

7. In the Enter The Object Names To Select box, key Administrators and click OK. The Administrators group appears in the Group Or User Names list in the Permissions For Documents dialog box.

8. With the Administrators group highlighted, select the Full Control checkbox in the Allow column, which causes the Change checkbox to be selected as well.

9. Using the same technique, add the Users group to the Group Or User Names list, and assign it the Allow Read permission only.

10. Take a screen shot of the Permissions For Support dialog box by pressing Alt+Prt Scr, and then paste the resulting image into the lab08_worksheet file in the page provided by pressing Ctrl+V.

11. Click OK to close the Permissions For Support dialog box.

12. Click OK to close the Advanced Sharing dialog box.

13. Click Close to close the Support Properties sheet.

14. Using one of the other student workstations in the classroom, open Windows Explorer, select Network, and browse to the Support share you just created on your computer.

15. When the Connect To Computer## dialog box appears, log on using the JAdams account you created in Lab 5.

16. Select one of the files in the Support/Migwiz folder and try to delete it.

Question 17	*Were you able to delete the file? Why or why not?*

17. Leave the windows on your workstation open for later exercises.

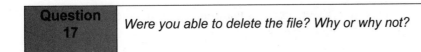

Exercise 8.5	Working with NTFS Permissions
Overview	You are a network administrator who has been assigned the task of setting up a kiosk computer on which various users can read Human Resources documents. You decide to use the Guest account on the computer for this purpose and provide that account with limited access to the documents, using NTFS permissions. In this exercise, you create NTFS permission assignments for a folder and view the effective permissions for the Guest user.
Completion time	20 minutes

1. Open the Computer Management console, as you did in Lab 5. Use the Local Users And Groups snap-in to enable the Guest user account, and assign it the password **P@ssw0rd**.

2. In Windows Explorer, select the Support folder you created in Exercise 8.3 and open its Properties sheet.

3. Click the Security tab.

4. Click Edit. After you confirm your action, the Permissions For Support dialog box appears.

5. Click Add. The Select Users Or Groups dialog box appears.

6. In the Enter The Object Names To Select box, key **Guest** and click OK. The Guest account is added to the Group Or User Names list in the Support Properties sheet.

7. Select the Guest account.

8. In the Permissions For Guest box, clear the Allow checkboxes for all except the Read and List Folder Contents permissions and then click Apply. The Guest account now has the Read and List Folder Contents permissions for the Support folder.

9. Click OK to close the Permissions For Support dialog box.

10. On the Support Properties sheet, click Advanced. The Advanced Security Settings For Support dialog box appears.

11. Click the Effective Permissions tab.

12. Click Select.

13. The Select Users Or Group dialog box appears.

14. Key **Guest** and click OK.

15. The currently effective permissions for the Guest user appear in the Effective Permissions box.

16. Take a screen shot of the Advanced Security Settings For Support dialog box by pressing Alt+Prt Scr, and then paste the resulting image into the lab08_worksheet file in the page provided by pressing Ctrl+V.

17. Log off of the computer.

LAB REVIEW QUESTIONS

Completion time	15 minutes

1. In Exercise 8.3, you compressed a folder on a Windows Vista drive to provide the user with more disk space. What would have been the result if the user's drive was formatted using the FAT32 file system instead of NTFS?

2. How would JAdams' remote access to the Support folder change if you modify the share permissions for the Support share by assigning the Full Control permission to the User group?

3. How would JAdams' remote access to the Support folder change if you modified the NTFS permissions by assigning him the Full Control permission to the User group?

4. How would JAdams' local access to the Support folder change if you modify the share permissions for the Support share by denying all permissions to the User group?

LAB CHALLENGE: ENCRYPTING FILES AND FOLDERS

Completion time	20 minutes

Calvin, the user from Exercise 8.3, calls the help desk and tells you that he is storing some extremely confidential company files on his computer. He is wondering whether there are some extraordinary security measures he can take to ensure that no one but the local Administrator account can access these files. Calvin also informs you that he has resolved his earlier disk space problem by archiving some files to DVD-ROMs. To complete this challenge, you must configure the Support folder on your computer to use the Encrypting File System and write out the procedure you used to perform this configuration. Then, test your work by attempting to access one of the files in the Support folder from another computer in the classroom.

LAB 9
CONFIGURING WINDOWS VISTA SECURITY

This lab contains the following exercises and activities:

Exercise 9.1	Installing Internet Information Server
Exercise 9.2	Testing IIS Connectivity
Exercise 9.3	Creating a Program Exception
Exercise 9.4	Creating Windows Firewall Rules
Lab Review	Questions
Lab Challenge	Deploying an FTP Server

BEFORE YOU BEGIN

Lab 9 assumes that setup has been completed as specified in the setup document, that your workstation has connectivity to the classroom network and other lab computers, and that you have completed the exercises in Labs 1 to 8. At this point, there should be two copies of Windows Vista installed on the student workstation, one clean installation that you performed in Lab 1 and one upgrade that you performed in Lab 3.

Before you start this lab, make sure you have the following information for your workstation:

Student workstation name (Computer##)	
Student account name (Student##)	

Working with Lab Worksheets

Each lab in this manual requires that you answer questions, shoot screen shots, or perform other activities that you will document in a worksheet named for the lab, such as lab01_worksheet.doc. You will find these worksheets on your student CD. As you perform the exercises in each lab, open the appropriate worksheet file using WordPad, fill in the required information, and save the file to your student folder on the SERVER01 computer. Your instructor will examine these worksheet files to assess your performance. At the end of each lab, make sure that you save your fully completed worksheet file to the server and not to your local drive.

The procedure for opening and saving a worksheet file is as follows:

1. Click Start, and then click Run. The Run dialog box appears.

2. In the Open text box, browse your student CD to find the worksheet for this lab. Click Open and then click OK.

3. The worksheet document opens in WordPad.

4. Complete all exercises in the worksheet.

5. In WordPad, choose Save As from the File menu. The Save As dialog box appears.

6. In the File Name text box, key
    \\server01\students\student##\lab##_worksheet_*yourname* (where student## contains your student number, lab## contains the number of the lab you're working on, and *yourname* is your last name).

SCENARIO

You are a Windows Vista desktop support technician for Contoso, Ltd., a company with workstations in a variety of different environments. You have been assigned the task of building a test Web server on the company's laboratory network. The Web server must host two separate Websites, one public site for Internet users and one intranet site for company employees. The server must also support FTP communications.

After completing this lab, you will be able to:

- Deploy Websites on Windows Vista

- Create exceptions in Windows Firewall

- Create rules for Windows Firewall

Estimated lab time: 125 minutes

Exercise 9.1	Installing Internet Information Server
Overview	Because this is only a test deployment, you will be using a Windows Vista computer to function as the Web server. In this exercise, you install Internet Information Services on your workstation and configure it to host two Websites.
Completion time	20 minutes

1. Turn on your workstation and, when the boot menu appears, select the clean copy of Windows Vista that you installed in Lab 3.

2. Log on using the student## account and the password **P@ssw0rd**.

3. Click Start, and then click Control Panel > Programs > Programs And Features. The Uninstall Or Change A Program window appears.

4. Click Turn Windows Features On Or Off. After confirming your action, the *Windows Features* page appears, as shown in Figure 9-1.

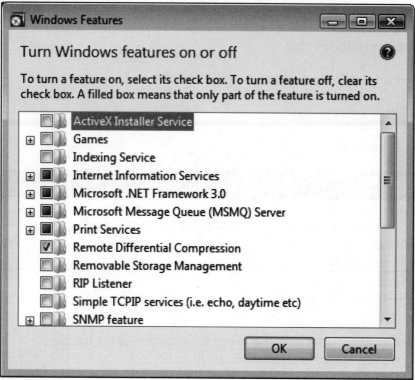

Figure 9-1
The Windows Features page

5. Expand the Internet Information Services folder.

6. Expand the Web Management Tools folder, and select the IIS Management Console checkbox.

7. Expand the World Wide Web folder.

8. Select the Common HTTP Features, Health And Diagnostics, and Security checkboxes.

9. Click OK. Windows Vista installs the selected IIS components.

10. Close the Programs And Features control panel window.

11. Click Start, and then click Control Panel > System And Maintenance > Administrative Tools. The Administrative Tools window appears.

12. Double-click Internet Information Services (IIS) Manager. After confirming your action, the Internet Information Services (IIS) Manager console appears, as shown in Figure 9-2.

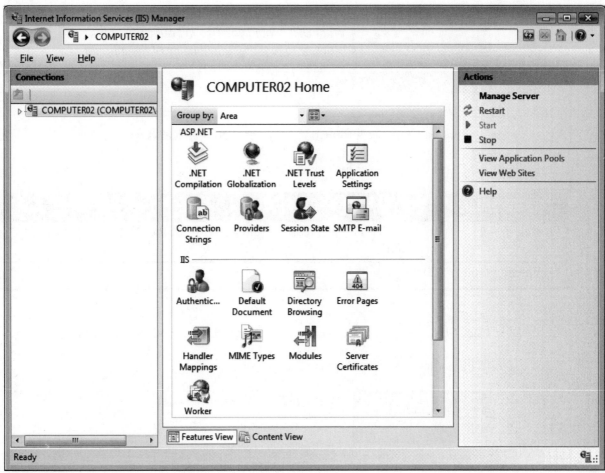

Figure 9-2
The Internet Information Services (IIS) Manager console

13. In the Connections pane (on the left), expand the Computer## container, and then expand the Web Sites folder.

14. Right-click the Web Sites folder and, from the context menu, select Add Web Site. The Add Web Site dialog box appears.

15. In the Web Site Name text box, key **Intranet**.

16. In the Physical Path text box, key **%SystemDrive%\inetpub\wwwroot**.

17. Change the value in the Port text box to **4444**.

18. Click OK. The new intranet Website appears in the Web sites folder in the Connections pane.

Question 1	What URL would you use in your computer's browser to test the functionality of the intranet Website you just created?

19. Close the Internet Information Services (IIS) Manager console.

20. Leave the computer logged on for the next exercise.

Exercise 9.2   Testing IIS Connectivity

Overview	In this exercise, you test the functionality of the Web server you just installed.
Completion time	20 minutes

1. Click Start, and then click Internet. An Internet Explorer window appears.

2. In the address box, key **http://127.0.0.1** and press Enter.

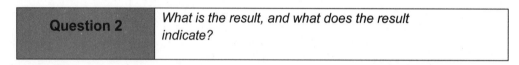

Question 2	What is the result, and what does the result indicate?

3. Next, test the intranet Website by using the URL you specified in Exercise 9.1.

Question 3	What is the result, and what does it signify?

4. Using another Windows Vista workstation in the classroom as your test client, open Internet Explorer and attempt to access the IIS Web server running on your computer by typing **http://computer##** (where ## is the number of your computer) in the address box and pressing Enter.

Question 4	What is the result?

5. Now, try to connect to the intranet Website from the test client computer.

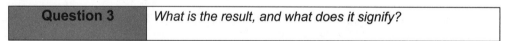

Question 5	What is the result?

6. Back on your computer, click Start, and then click Control Panel > Security > Windows Firewall. The Windows Firewall window appears.

7. Click Change Settings. After you confirm the action, the Windows Firewall Settings dialog box appears, as shown in Figure 9-3.

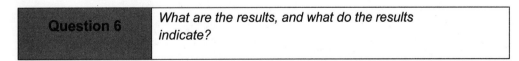

Windows Firewall Settings

General | Exceptions | Advanced

✓ Windows Firewall is helping to protect your computer

Windows Firewall can help prevent hackers or malicious software from gaining access to your computer through the Internet or a network.

⦿ **On (recommended)**

This setting blocks all outside sources from connecting to this computer, except for those unblocked on the Exceptions tab.

☐ **Block all incoming connections**

Select this option when you connect to less secure networks. All exceptions will be ignored and you will not be notified when Windows Firewall blocks programs.

○ **Off (not recommended)**

Avoid using this setting. Turning off Windows Firewall will make this computer more vulnerable to hackers or malicious software.

Tell me more about these settings

OK | Cancel | Apply

Figure 9-3
The Windows Firewall Settings dialog box

8. Select the Off radio button and click Apply.

9. Return to the test client computer, and try again to access both of the sites on the Web server using Internet Explorer.

Question 6	What are the results, and what do the results indicate?

10. Clear the Internet Explorer cache on the test client computer by clicking Tools > Internet Options. The Internet Options dialog box appears.

11. Under Browsing History, click the Delete button. The Delete Browsing History dialog box appears.

12. Under Temporary Internet Files, click Delete Files. A Delete Files message box appears, prompting you to confirm your action.

13. Click Yes, and then click Close and OK to close the two dialog boxes.

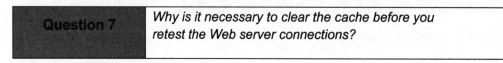

Question 7	*Why is it necessary to clear the cache before you retest the Web server connections?*

14. Back on your computer in the Windows Firewall Settings dialog box, select the On radio button and click OK.

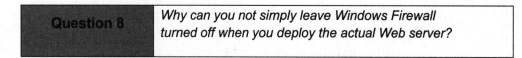

Question 8	*Why can you not simply leave Windows Firewall turned off when you deploy the actual Web server?*

15. Leave the windows open for the next exercise.

Exercise 9.3	Creating a Program Exception
Overview	Windows Firewall is preventing clients from connecting to the Web server. To enable client access, you will create an exception that opens up the port that the Web server uses.
Completion time	20 minutes

1. Open the Windows Firewall Settings dialog box on your workstation, and click the Exceptions tab. See Figure 9-4.

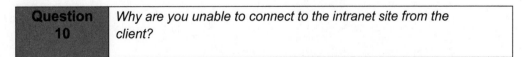

Figure 9-4
The Exceptions tab of the Windows Firewall Settings dialog box

2. Scroll down the Program Or Port list, select the World Wide Web Services (HTTP) checkbox, and then click OK.

3. Return to the test client computer and attempt to connect to the default Website.

Question 9	*Why are you now able to connect to the Website from the client?*

4. Now test the connection to the intranet Website.

Question 10	*Why are you unable to connect to the intranet site from the client?*

5. Open the Windows Firewall Settings dialog box. On the Exceptions tab, clear the World Wide Web Services (HTTP) checkbox, and then click OK.

6. Leave the remaining windows open for the next exercise.

Exercise 9.4	Creating Windows Firewall Rules
Overview	The program exception that you created in Exercise 9.3 enables clients to access the default Website hosted by your Web server, but not the intranet Website. In this exercise, you use the Windows Firewall With Advanced Security console to create rules that will enable clients to access both Websites.
Completion time	20 minutes

1. On your Web server workstation, open the Administrative Tools window.

2. Double-click Windows Firewall With Advanced Security. The Windows Firewall With Advanced Security console appears, as shown in Figure 9-5.

3. In the left pane, click Inbound Rules. The list of default inbound rules appears in the center pane.

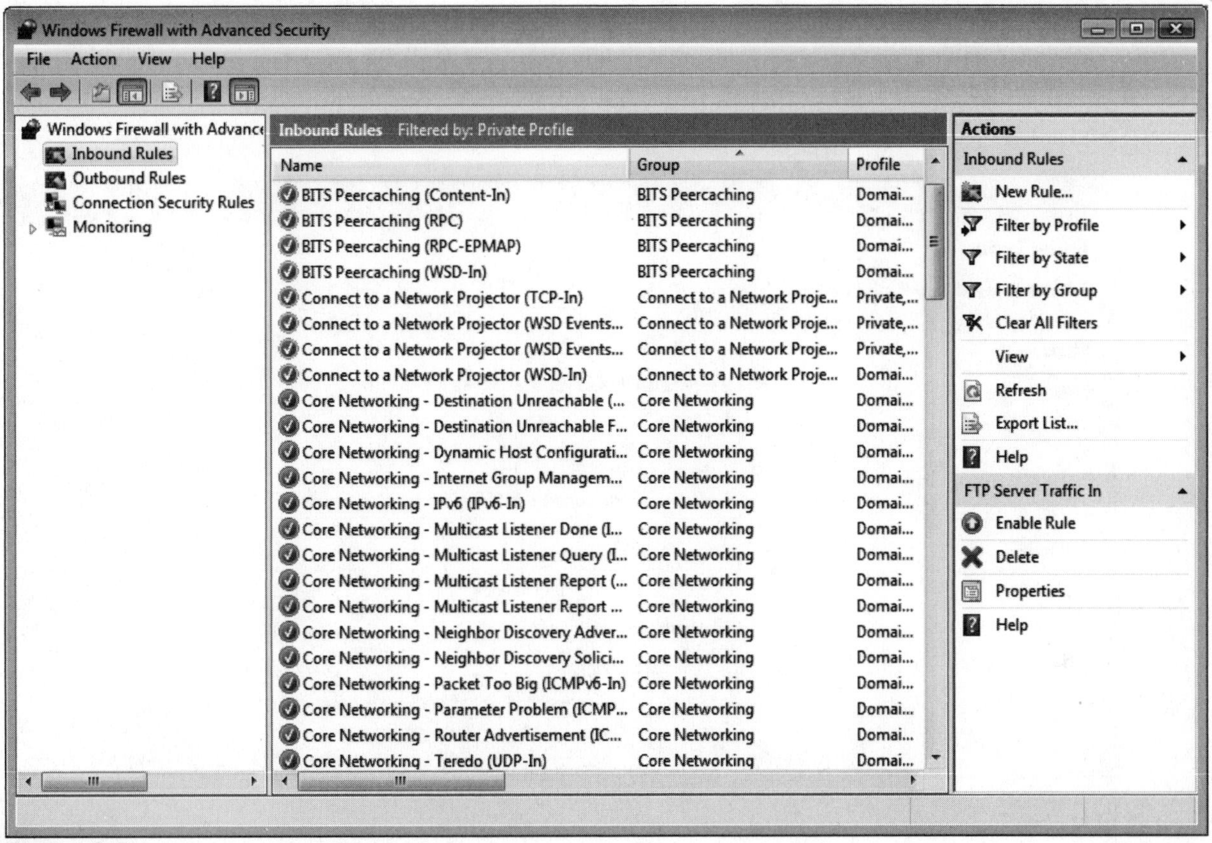

Figure 9-5
The Windows Firewall With Advanced Security console

4. Scroll down to the bottom of the list and locate the rules for World Wide Web Services HTTP Traffic In.

Question 11	Why are there two separate rules for the World Wide Web Services?

5. Double-click each of the two rules and examine their properties.

Question 12	How do the properties of the two rules differ?

6. In the Actions pane (on the right side), click Filter By Profile and, from the context menu, select Filter By Private Profile.

Question 13	What happens to the list of rules?

7. In the left pane, right-click the Inbound Rules icon and, from the context menu, select New Rule. The New Inbound Rule Wizard launches, and the *Rule Type* page appears. See Figure 9-6.

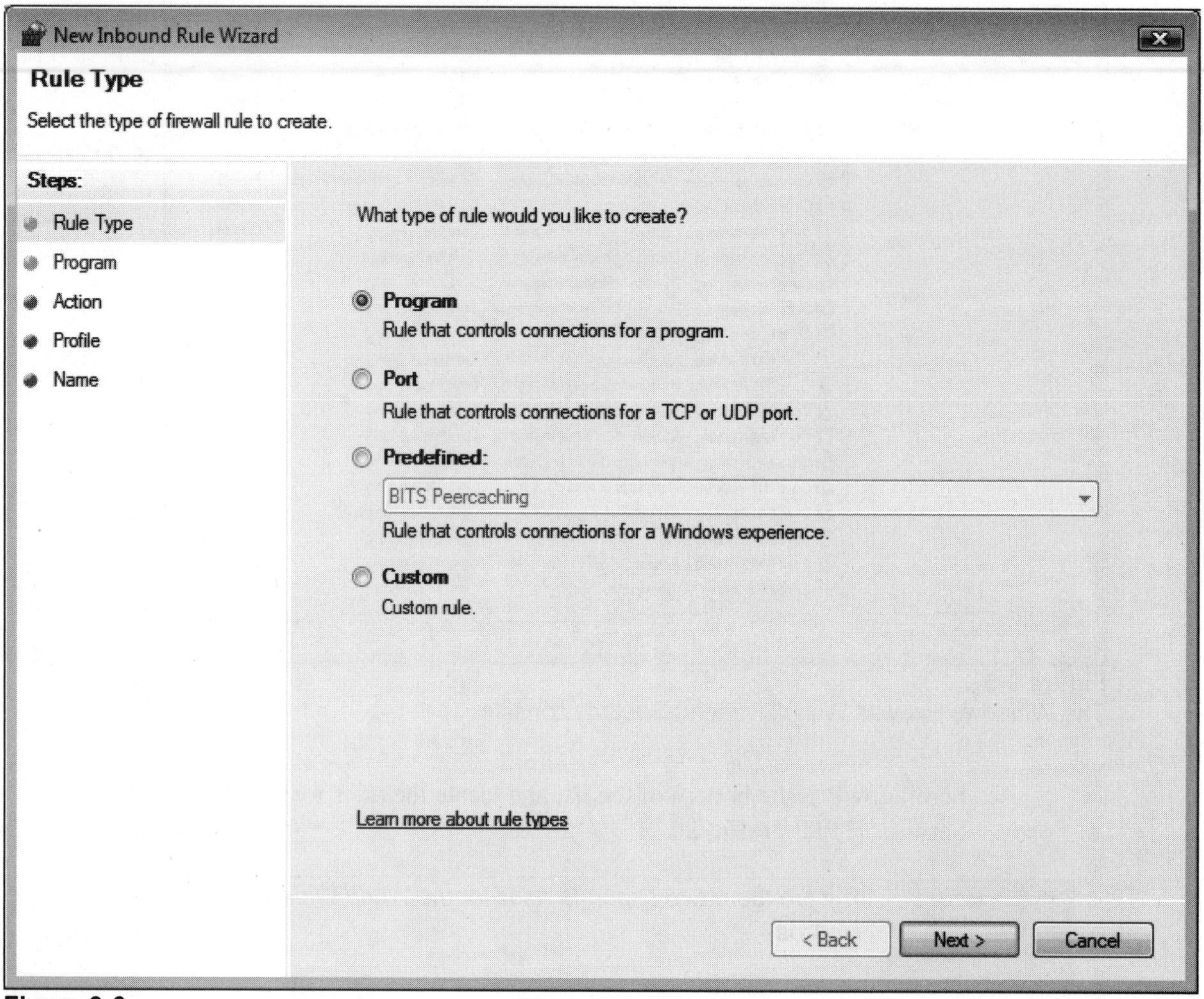

New Inbound Rule Wizard ☒

Rule Type

Select the type of firewall rule to create.

Steps:
- Rule Type
- Program
- Action
- Profile
- Name

What type of rule would you like to create?

⦿ **Program**
  Rule that controls connections for a program.

○ **Port**
  Rule that controls connections for a TCP or UDP port.

○ **Predefined:**

  | BITS Peercaching ▼ |

  Rule that controls connections for a Windows experience.

○ **Custom**
  Custom rule.

<u>Learn more about rule types</u>

[< Back] [Next >] [Cancel]

Figure 9-6
The New Inbound Rule Wizard

8. Select the Port option and click Next. The *Protocol And Ports* page appears.

9. Leave the default TCP and Specific Local Ports options selected. In the Specific Local Ports text box. Key **80, 4444** and click Next. The *Action* page appears.

10. Leave the default Allow The Connection option selected and click Next. The *Profile* page appears.

11. Clear the Domain and Public checkboxes, leaving only the Private checkbox selected, and then click Next. The *Name* page appears.

12. In the Name text box, key **Lab Web Server – Ports 80 & 4444** and click Finish. The wizard creates and enables the new rule and then adds it to the Inbound Rules list.

13. Take a screen shot of the Properties sheet for the new rule you created by pressing Alt+Prt Scr, and then paste the resulting image into the lab09_worksheet file in the page provided by pressing Ctrl+V.

14. Return to the test client computer, and repeat your attempts to connect to both Web servers.

	What are the results, and why are they different from the results you experienced with the program exception?

15. Log off of the computer.

LAB REVIEW QUESTIONS

Completion time	**15 minutes**

1. In Exercise 9.2, you were initially unable to connect to your computer's Web server using a browser on another computer. Based only on what you knew at the time, list three possible reasons why the connection could have failed.

2. In Exercise 9.2, what other test could you perform to prove that it was your computer's firewall that was blocking the connection and not the firewall on the computer you were using as a client?

3. How would the creation of the exception you performed in Exercise 9.3 affect the World Wide Web Services HTTP Traffic In rules you examined in the Windows Firewall With Advanced Security console?

4. How would the rule creation procedure you performed in Exercise 9.4 differ if you wanted to restrict client access to the intranet Website to computers on the local network only?

LAB CHALLENGE: DEPLOYING AN FTP SERVER

Completion time	30 minutes

The test server you have created in this lab must support FTP as well as Web clients, but only for clients on the local network. To perform this challenge, complete the following tasks.

1. Install the FTP Server and FTP Management Console modules into IIS on your workstation, and activate the default FTP site.

2. Copy some files from the C:\support folder to the FTP root folder.

3. Create a new rule that opens the ports needed for incoming FTP traffic, allowing access only to clients on the local network. List the settings you used to create the rule in the following table.

Wizard Page	Settings
Rule Type	
Program	
Protocol And Ports	
Scope	
Action	
Profile	
Name	

4. From a test client computer, use Internet Explorer to access the FTP site with the URL **http://Computer##**.

5. Take a screen shot of the Internet Explorer window showing the FTP site by pressing Alt+Prt Scr, and then paste the resulting image into the lab09_worksheet file in the page provided by pressing Ctrl+V.

LAB 10
MONITORING WINDOWS VISTA PERFORMANCE

This lab contains the following exercises and activities:

Exercise 10.1   Using Performance Monitor

Exercise 10.2   Logging Performance Data

Exercise 10.3   Creating a Performance Counter Alert

Lab Review   Questions

Lab Challenge   Viewing a Performance Counter Log

BEFORE YOU BEGIN

Lab 10 assumes that setup has been completed as specified in the setup document, that your workstation has connectivity to the classroom network and other lab computers, and that you have completed the exercises in Labs 1 to 9. At this point, there should be two copies of Windows Vista installed on the student workstation, one clean installation that you performed in Lab 1 and one upgrade that you performed in Lab 3.

Before you start this lab, make sure you have the following information for your workstation:

Student workstation name (Computer##)	
Student account name (Student##)	

Working with Lab Worksheets

Each lab in this manual requires that you answer questions, shoot screen shots, or perform other activities that you will document in a worksheet named for the lab, such as lab01_worksheet.doc. You will find these worksheets on your student CD. As you perform the exercises in each lab, open the appropriate worksheet file using WordPad, fill in the required information, and save the file to your student folder on the SERVER01 computer. Your instructor will examine these worksheet files to assess your performance. at the end of each lab, make sure thatyou save your fully completed worksheet file to the server and not to your local drive.

The procedure for opening and saving a worksheet file is as follows:

1. Click Start, and then click Run. The Run dialog box appears.

2. In the Open text, browse your student CD to find the worksheet for this lab. Click Open and then click OK.

3. The worksheet document opens in WordPad.

4. Complete all exercises in the worksheet.

5. In WordPad, choose Save As from the File menu. The Save As dialog box appears.

6. In the File Name text box, key **\\server01\students\student##\lab##_worksheet_*yourname*** (where student## contains your student number, lab## contains the number of the lab you're working on, and *yourname* is your last name).

SCENARIO

You are a newly hired desktop technician for Contoso, Ltd. and have been assigned to work on a long-term test deployment of some new Windows Vista workstations. Your job is to track the computers' performance levels over the course of a week and determine which components, if any, are negatively affecting system performance.

After completing this lab, you will be able to:

- Automatically deploy operating system updates on Windows Vista

- Monitor Windows Vista performance levels

- Create Windows Vista performance logs and alerts

Estimated lab time: 120 minutes

Exercise 10.1	Using Performance Monitor
Overview	The desktop support technicians at Contoso, Ltd. routinely use the Performance Monitor tool to examine the performance levels of Windows Vista workstations. However, each technician uses Performance Monitor in a different way. The IT director wants to create a standard set of performance counters that are easily visible in a single Performance Monitor line graph that would enable the support staff to compare the performance levels of different computer models. You have been given the task of selecting the performance counters for this standard Performance Monitor configuration and testing their visibility on the graph.
Completion time	30 minutes

1. Turn on your workstation and, when the boot menu appears, select the clean copy of Windows Vista that you installed in Lab 3.

2. Log on using the student## account and the password **P@ssw0rd**.

3. Click Start, and then click Control Panel. The Control Panel window appears.

4. Click System And Maintenance, and then click Administrative Tools. The Administrative Tools window appears.

5. Double-click Reliability And Performance Monitor. Click Continue in the User Account Control dialog box, and the Reliability And Performance Monitor window appears.

6. In the scope pane, click Performance Monitor. The Performance Monitor window appears, as shown in Figure 10-1.

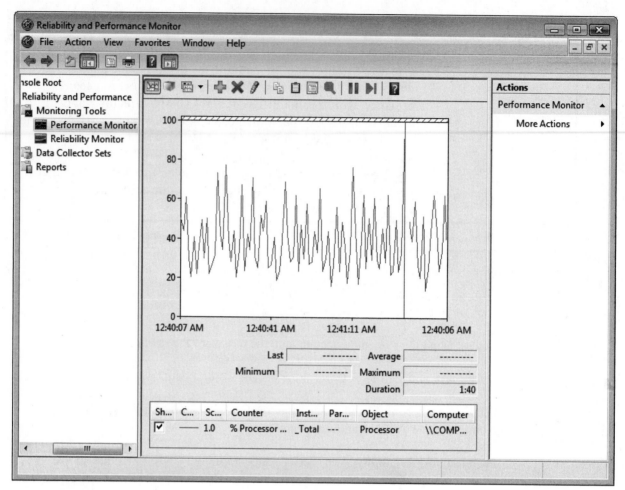

Figure 10-1
Performance Monitor window

Question 1	What counter appears in the Performance Monitor display by default?

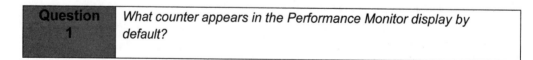

7. Remove the default counter from the Performance Monitor graph by selecting it in the legend (below the line graph) and clicking the Delete button in the toolbar.

8. Click the Add button in the toolbar. The Add Counters dialog box appears.

9. In the Available Counters list, expand the Server Work Queues entry, as shown in Figure 10-2.

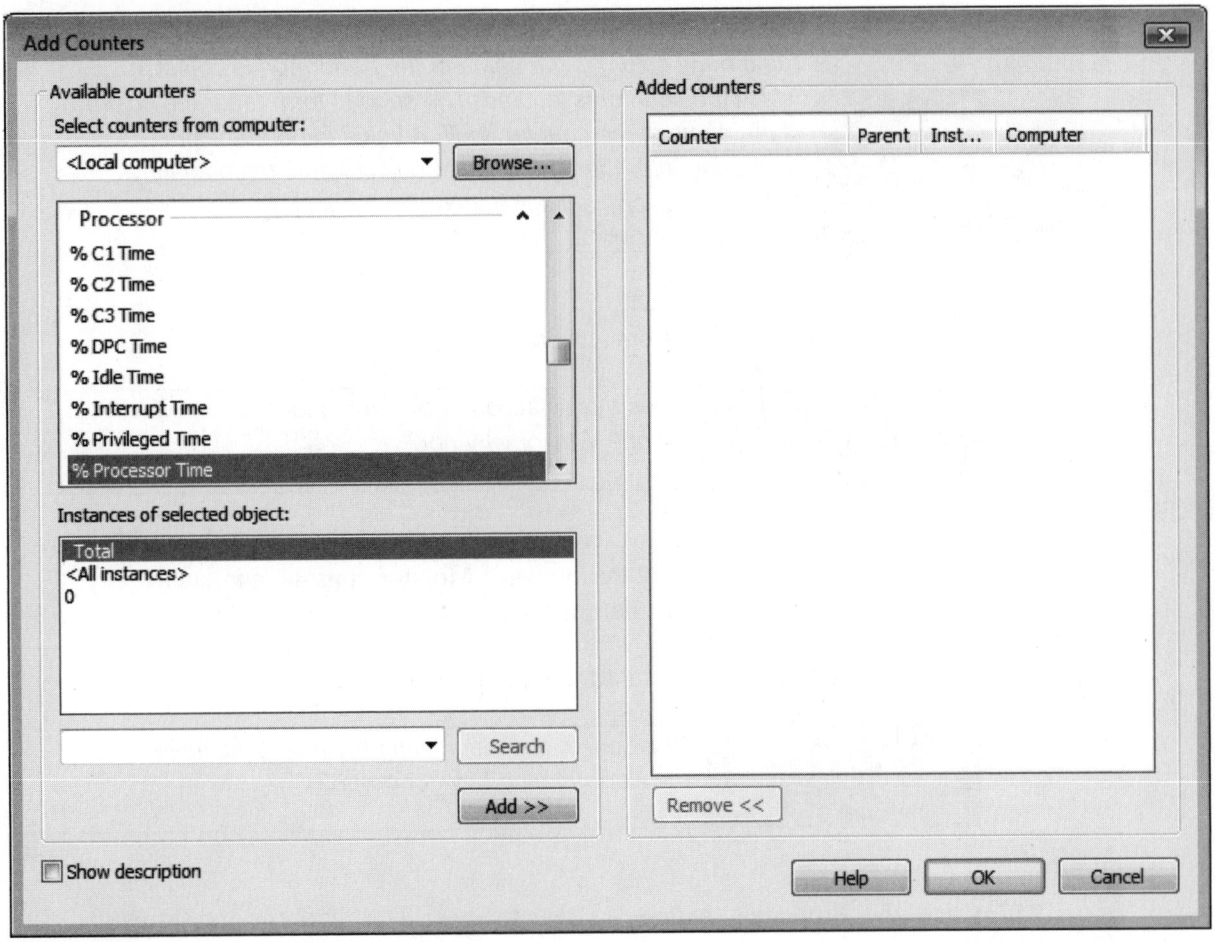

Figure 10-2
Add Counters dialog box

10. Select the Queue Length counter.

11. In the Instances Of Selected Object list, select 0, and then click Add.

12. Click OK to close the dialog box.

Question 2	What happens?

13. Using the same process, add the following additional counters to the graph:

- System: Processor Queue Length
- Memory: Page Faults/Sec
- Memory: Pages/Sec
- PhysicalDisk (_Total): Current Disk Queue Length

For each of the performance counters listed, the first term (before the colon) is the name of the performance object in which the counter is located. The second term (after the colon) is the name of the counter itself. A value in parentheses appearing after the performance object name (immediately before the colon) is the instance of the counter.

14. Click OK to close the Add Counters dialog box.

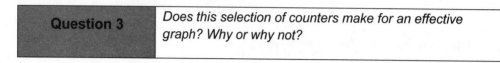

Question 3 *Does this selection of counters make for an effective graph? Why or why not?*

15. Minimize the Reliability And Performance Monitor console, and launch any three new programs from the Start menu.

16. Maximize the Reliability And Performance Monitor console.

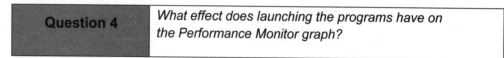

Question 4 *What effect does launching the programs have on the Performance Monitor graph?*

17. Click the Properties button on the toolbar. The Performance Monitor Properties sheet appears.

18. Click the Graph tab, as shown in Figure 10-3.

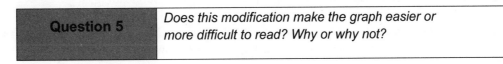

Figure 10-3
Graph tab of the Performance Monitor Properties sheet

19. In the Vertical Scale box, change the value of the Maximum field to **200** and click OK.

Question 5	*Does this modification make the graph easier or more difficult to read? Why or why not?*

20. Take a screen shot of the Performance Monitor window showing the line graph by pressing Alt+Prt Scr, and then paste the resulting image into the lab10_worksheet file in the page provided by pressing Ctrl+V.

21. From the console's Window menu, select New Window. A new Console Root window appears.

22. Display the Performance Monitor graph in the new window.

23. Click the Add button, and add the following counters to the Performance Monitor graph:

- Network Interface (All Instances): Packets/Sec
- Network Interface (All Instances): Output Queue Length
- Server: Bytes Total/Sec

24. Click OK to close the Add Counters dialog box.

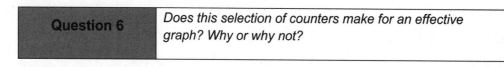

Question 6	Does this selection of counters make for an effective graph? Why or why not?

25. Leave the Reliability And Performance Monitor console open for the next exercise.

Exercise 10.2	Logging Performance Data
Overview	To properly gauge the performance level of a computer, it is helpful to have a baseline reading that you've taken under normal operating conditions that you can use to compare with the levels when the computer is under the stress of a work load. You have been given the task of taking baseline performance level readings on a new computer using the Reliability And Performance Monitor console. In this exercise, you use the Data Collector Sets tool to create a counter log for the computer, saving the baseline levels to a file for later examination.
Completion time	30 minutes

1. In the Relability And Performance Monitor console, expand the Data Collector Sets node and select the User Defined subheading.

2. On the Action menu, point to New and select Data Collector Set. The Create New Data Collector Set Wizard appears, as shown in Figure 10-4.

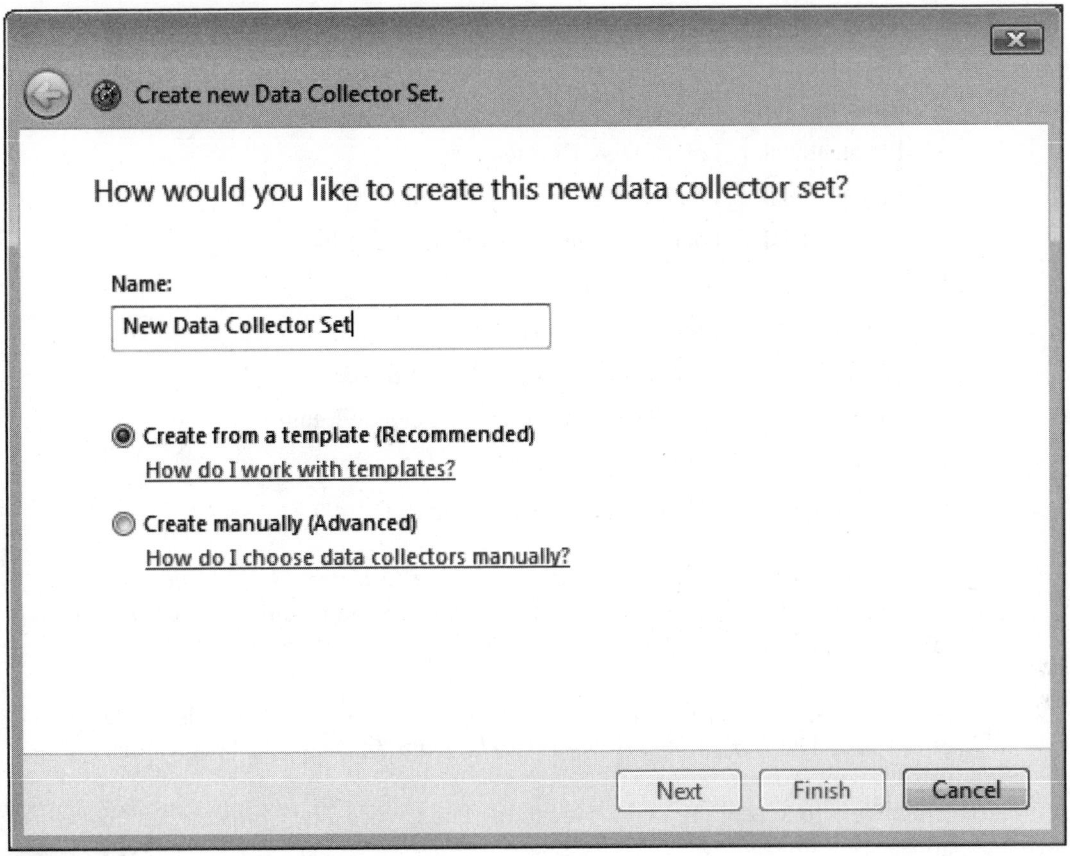

Figure 10-4
Create New Data Collector Set Wizard

3. In the Name text box, key **Computer*xx* Baseline**, where *xx* is the number assigned to the computer.

4. Select the Create Manually radio button and click Next. The *What Type Of Data Do You Want To Include?* page appears.

5. With the Create Data Logs option selected, select the Performance Counter checkbox and click Next. The *Which Performance Counters Would You Like To Log?* page appears.

6. Click the Add button. Using the same procedure from Exercise 10.1, add the following counters:

   • Processor (_Total): % Processor time

   • Processor (_Total): Interrupts/sec

   • System: Processor Queue Length

   • Server Work Queues (0): Queue Length

   • Memory: Page Faults/Sec

   • Memory: Pages/Sec

- Memory: Available Bytes
- Memory: Committed Bytes
- Memory: Pool Nonpaged Bytes
- PhysicalDisk (_Total): Disk Bytes/sec
- PhysicalDisk (_Total): Avg. Disk Bytes/Transfer
- PhysicalDisk (_Total): Current Disk Queue Length
- PhysicalDisk (_Total): % Disk Time
- LogicalDisk (_Total): % Free Space
- Network Interface (All Instances): Bytes Total/sec
- Network Interface (All Instances): Output Queue Length
- Server: Bytes Total/Sec

7. Click OK to close the Add Counters dialog box.

8. Take a screen shot of the *Which Performance Counters Would You Like To Log?* page by pressing Alt+Prt Scr, and then paste the resulting image into the lab10_worksheet file in the page provided by pressing Ctrl+V.

9. Set the Sample Interval value to 10 and the units value to Seconds, and then click Next. The *Where Would You Like The Data To Be Saved?* page appears.

10. Click Next to accept the default location. The *Create The Collector Set?* page appears.

11. Select the Open Properties For This Data Collector Set option and click Finish. The Computerxx Baseline Properties sheet appears, as shown in Figure 10-5.

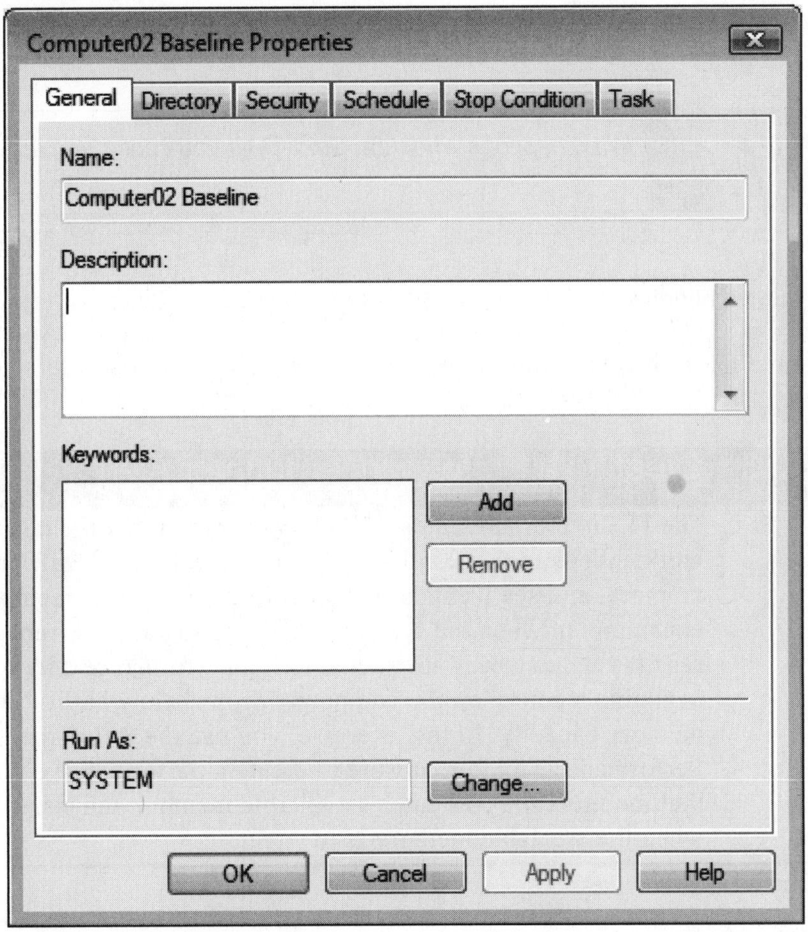

Figure 10-5
Computerxx Baseline Properties sheet

12. Click the Schedule tab, and then click Add. The Folder Action dialog box appears.

13. Make sure that today's date appears in the Beginning Date drop-down list.

14. Select the Expiration Date checkbox, and make sure that today's date appears in the Expiration Date drop-down list.

15. In the Launch box, set the Start Time value for five minutes from now. Clear all of the checkboxes except the one for the current day of the week, and then click OK.

16. Click the Stop Condition tab.

17. Select the Overall Duration checkbox, set the value for 10 Minutes, and then click OK.

18. The DataCollector01 Performance Counter log appears in the console's details pane.

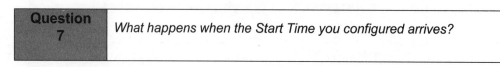

Question 7	What happens when the Start Time you configured arrives?

19. Wait ten minutes for the logging process to complete.

20. Leave the Reliability And Performance Monitor console open for the next exercise.

Exercise 10.3	Creating a Performance Counter Alert
Overview	The IT director at Contoso, Ltd. is concerned that the new workstations in the test deployment might not have sufficient memory, and she wants to gather information about memory consumption when the systems are operating at peak capacity. As a result, you have been instructed to log performance data when the available memory on the computers drops below half of the installed memory capacity. In this exercise, you use the Reliability And Performance Monitor console to create a performance counter alert that monitors the computer's available memory and starts logging when the available memory is low.
Completion time	30 minutes

1. In the Relability And Performance Monitor console, expand the Data Collector Sets node and select the User Defined subheading.

2. Using the same procedure as in Exercise 10.2, create a performance counter data collector set called **Computerxx Memory Log**, and add the following counters.

   - Memory: Available MBytes
   - Memory: Cache Bytes
   - Memory Cache Faults/Sec
   - Memory: Committed Bytes
   - Memory: Page Faults/Sec
   - Memory: Pages/Sec
   - Memory: Pool Nonpaged Bytes
   - Memory: System Code Total Bytes

3. Open the Computerxx Memory Log Properties sheet, and click the Stop Condition tab. Select the Overall Duration checkbox, set the duration to 60 Minutes, and then click OK.

4. Select the User Defined node and, from the Action menu, point to New and select Data Collector Set. The Create New Data Collector Set Wizard appears.

5. In the Name text box, key **Computerxx Memory Alert**, where *xx* is the number assigned to the computer.

6. Select the Create Manually radio button and click Next. The *What Type Of Data Do You Want To Include?* page appears.

7. Select the Performance Counter Alert option and click Next. The *Which Performance Counters Would You Like To Monitor?* page appears.

8. Click the Add button. Using the same procedure from Exercise 10.1, add the Memory: Available Mbytes counter and click OK.

9. Set the Alert When value to Below and the Limit value to half of the computer's installed memory (in megabytes), and then click Next. The *Create The Data Collector Set?* page appears.

If you don't know how much memory is installed in the computer, you can find out by opening the Welcome Center window from the Start menu.

10. Select the Save And Close option, and click Finish. The new alert appears in the scope pane.

11. Select Computerxx Memory Alert in the scope pane.

12. Right-click the DataCollector01 collector set in the detail pane and, from the context menu, select Properties. The DataCollector01 Properties sheet appears, as shown in Figure 10-6.

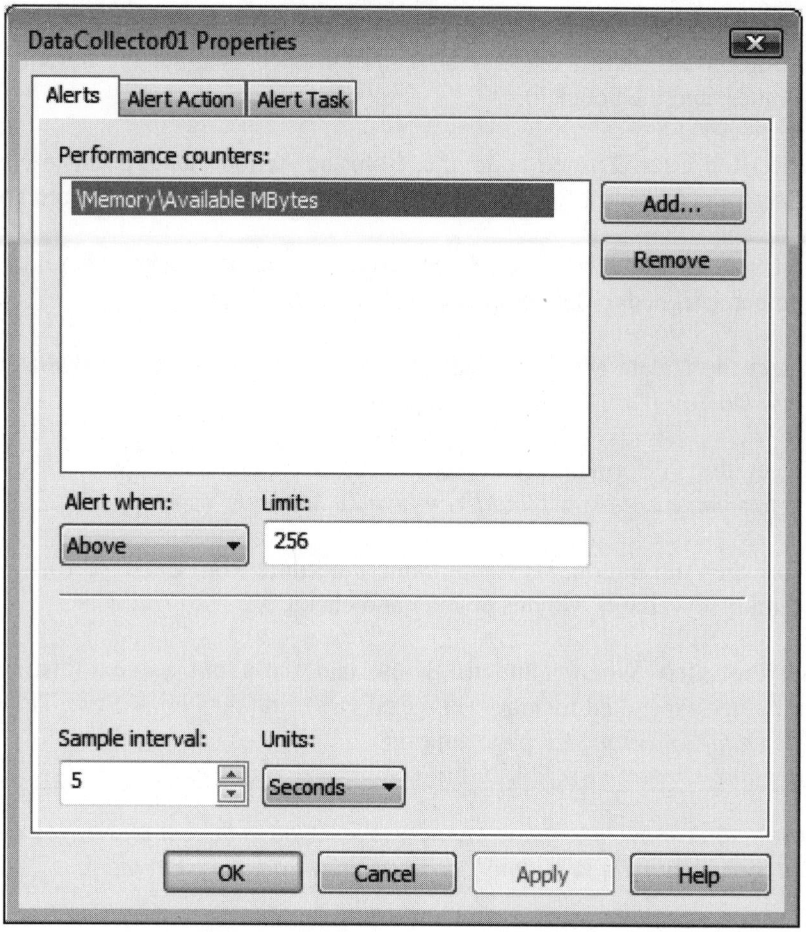

Figure 10-6
DataCollector01 Properties sheet

13. On the General tab, set the Sample Interval value to 10 Seconds.

14. Click the Alert Action tab.

15. Select the Log An Entry In The Application Event Log checkbox.

16. From the Start A Data Collector Set drop-down list, select Computerxx Memory Log.

17. Take a screen shot of the Alert Action tab by pressing Alt+Prt Scr, and then paste the resulting image into the lab10_worksheet file in the page provided by pressing Ctrl+V.

18. Click OK.

19. Select the Computerxx Memory Alert collector set you just created in the scope pane and, from the Action menu, select Start.

Question 8	What will happen if the computer's available memory drops below the threshold you specified in the performance counter alert collector set you created?

LAB REVIEW QUESTIONS

Completion time	10 minutes

1. In Exercise 10.1, how would using the report view instead of the line graph view affect the compatibility of the performance counters you select?

2. When creating a performance counter collector set, under what circumstances would it be necessary to specify a user name and password in the Run As section of the collector set's Properties sheet?

LAB CHALLENGE: VIEWING A PERFORMANCE COUNTER LOG

Completion time	20 minutes

In Exercise 10.2, you created a performance counter collector set for the purpose of gathering baseline performance data for your Windows Vista computer. To complete this challenge, you must use the Reliability And Performance Monitor console to display the data you gathered for the counters in the Memory performance object that you collected. Write out the procedure you used to display the data. Take a screen shot of the console showing the collector set data by pressing Alt+Prt Scr, and then paste the resulting image into the lab10_worksheet file in the page provided by pressing Ctrl+V.

LAB 11
USING REMOTE ACCESS

This lab contains the following exercises and activities:

Exercise 11.1	Configuring the Remote Access Client
Exercise 11.2	Creating a Remote Assistance Invitation
Exercise 11.3	Providing Remote Assistance
Exercise 11.4	Connecting with Remote Desktop
Lab Review	Questions
Lab Challenge	Remotely Configuring Windows Update

BEFORE YOU BEGIN

Lab 11 assumes that setup has been completed as specified in the setup document, that your workstation has connectivity to the classroom network and other lab computers, and that you have completed the exercises in Labs 1 to 10. At this point, there should be two copies of Windows Vista installed on the student workstation, one clean installation that you performed in Lab 1 and one upgrade that you performed in Lab 3.

Before you start this lab, make sure you have the following information for your workstation:

Student workstation name (Computer##)	
Student account name (Student##)	

For this lab, you must have a partner working on another Windows Vista workstation on the classroom network. Both partners must first complete Exercise 11.1 on their own computers individually. Then one partner begins Exercise 11.2 while the other partner performs Exercise 11.3, waiting until the Remote Assistance invitation has been created. After establishing a Remote Assistance connection between the two computers, the partners complete Exercises 11.2 and 11.3, respectively, and then switch roles, with each beginning the other exercise. Once both partners have completed Exercise 11.2 and Exercise 11.3, they should both complete Exercise 11.4, one at a time, with each connecting to the other partner's computer using Remote Desktop.

Working with Lab Worksheets

Each lab in this manual requires that you answer questions, shoot screen shots, or perform other activities that you are to document in a worksheet named for the lab, such as lab01_worksheet.doc. You will find these worksheets on your student CD. As you perform the exercises in each lab, open the appropriate worksheet file using WordPad, fill in the required information, and save the file to your student folder on the SERVER01 computer. Your instructor will examine these worksheet files to assess your performance. at the end of each lab, make sure that, you save your fully completed worksheet file to the server and not to your local drive.

The procedure for opening and saving a worksheet file is as follows:

1. Click Start, and then click Run. The Run dialog box appears.

2. In the Open text box, browse your student CD to find the worksheet for this lab. Click Open and then click OK.

3. The worksheet document opens in WordPad.

4. Complete all exercises in the worksheet.

5. In WordPad, choose Save As from the File menu. The Save As dialog box appears.

6. In the File Name text box, key
   \\server01\students\student##\lab##_worksheet_*yourname* (where student## contains your student number, lab## contains the number of the lab you're working on, and *yourname* is your last name).

SCENARIO

You are a newly hired desktop technician for Contoso, Ltd., working on a long-term test deployment of new Windows Vista workstations. You and a colleague have been given the task of testing the Windows Vista Remote Assistance and Remote Desktop technologies to determine whether they can be used satisfactorily for technical support and remote administration purposes.

After completing this lab, you will be able to:

- Configure the Windows Vista Remote Access technologies

- Create a Remote Assistance invitation

- Connect to another computer using Remote Assistance

- Use Remote Deskop to connect to an unattended computer

Estimated lab time: 120 minutes

Exercise 11.1	Configuring the Remote Access Client
Overview	Before you can test the Remote Assistance and Remote Desktop programs, both of the Windows Vista computers involved must be configured to allow secured connections to occur. In this exercise, both you and your colleague configure the Remote Access settings on your individual computers.
Completion time	10 minutes

1. Turn on your workstation and, when the boot menu appears, select the clean copy of Windows Vista that you installed in Lab 3.

2. Log on using the student## account and the password **P@ssw0rd**.

3. Click Start, and then click Control Panel. The Control Panel window appears.

4. Click System And Maintenance, and then click System. The System window appears.

5. Click Remote Settings. After you confirm your action, the System Properties sheet appears with the Remote tab selected, as shown in Figure 11-1.

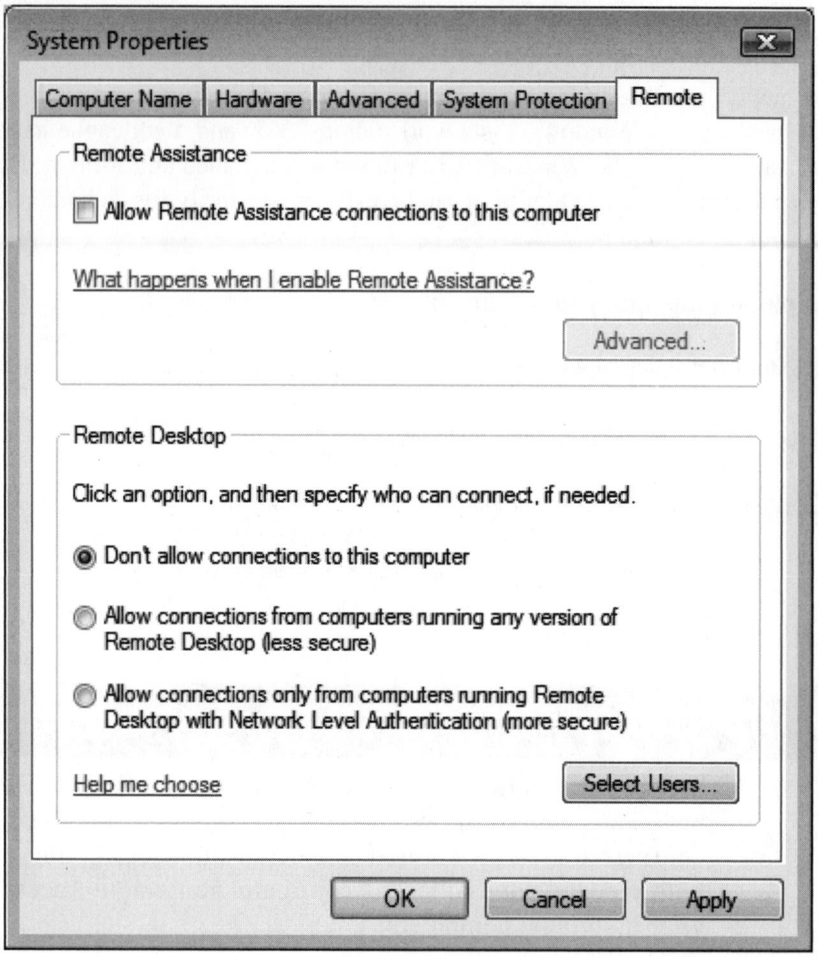

Figure 11-1
System Properties sheet

6. Select the Allow Remote Assistance Connections To This Computer checkbox. In the Remote Desktop box, select the Allow Connections From Computers Running Any Version Of Remote Desktop option and click Advanced. The Remote Assistance Settings dialog box appears, as shown in Figure 11-2.

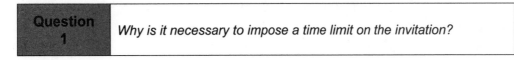

Figure 11-2
Remote Assistance Settings dialog box

7. Make sure that the Allow This Computer To Be Controlled Remotely checkbox is selected. In the Invitations box, set the maximum amount of time that invitations can remain open to 24 Hours and click OK.

Question 1	Why is it necessary to impose a time limit on the invitation?

8. Click OK to close the System Properties dialog box.

9. Open the User Accounts control panel. Create an administrative account for your partner using the account name Student*xx*, where *xx* is your partner's student number, and assign it the password **P@ssw0rd**.

10. Leave the computer logged on for the next exercise.

131

Exercise 11.2	Creating a Remote Assistance Invitation
Overview	To test Remote Assistance technology in Windows Vista, both partners must be present at their computers. In this exercise, you function as the user requesting help from a desktop technician by creating a Remote Assistance invitation and allowing your colleague to connect to your workstation.
Completion time	30 minutes

1. Click Start, and then click Help And Support. The Windows Help And Support window appears, as shown in Figure 11-3.

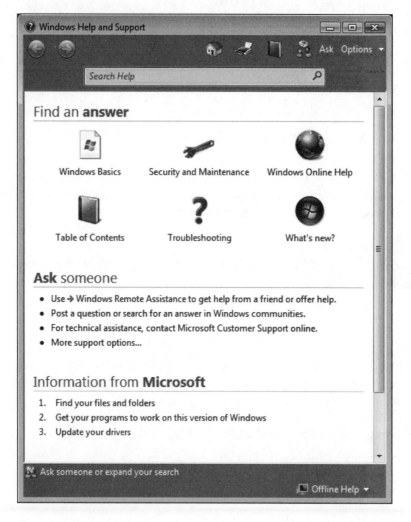

Figure 11-3
Windows Help and Support window

2. Under Ask Someone, click the Windows Remote Assistance link. The Windows Remote Assistance Wizard appears.

3. Click Invite Someone You Trust To Help You. The *How Do You Want To Invite Someone To Help You?* page appears.

4. Click Save The Invitation As A File. The *Save The Invitation As A File* page appears, as shown in Figure 11-4.

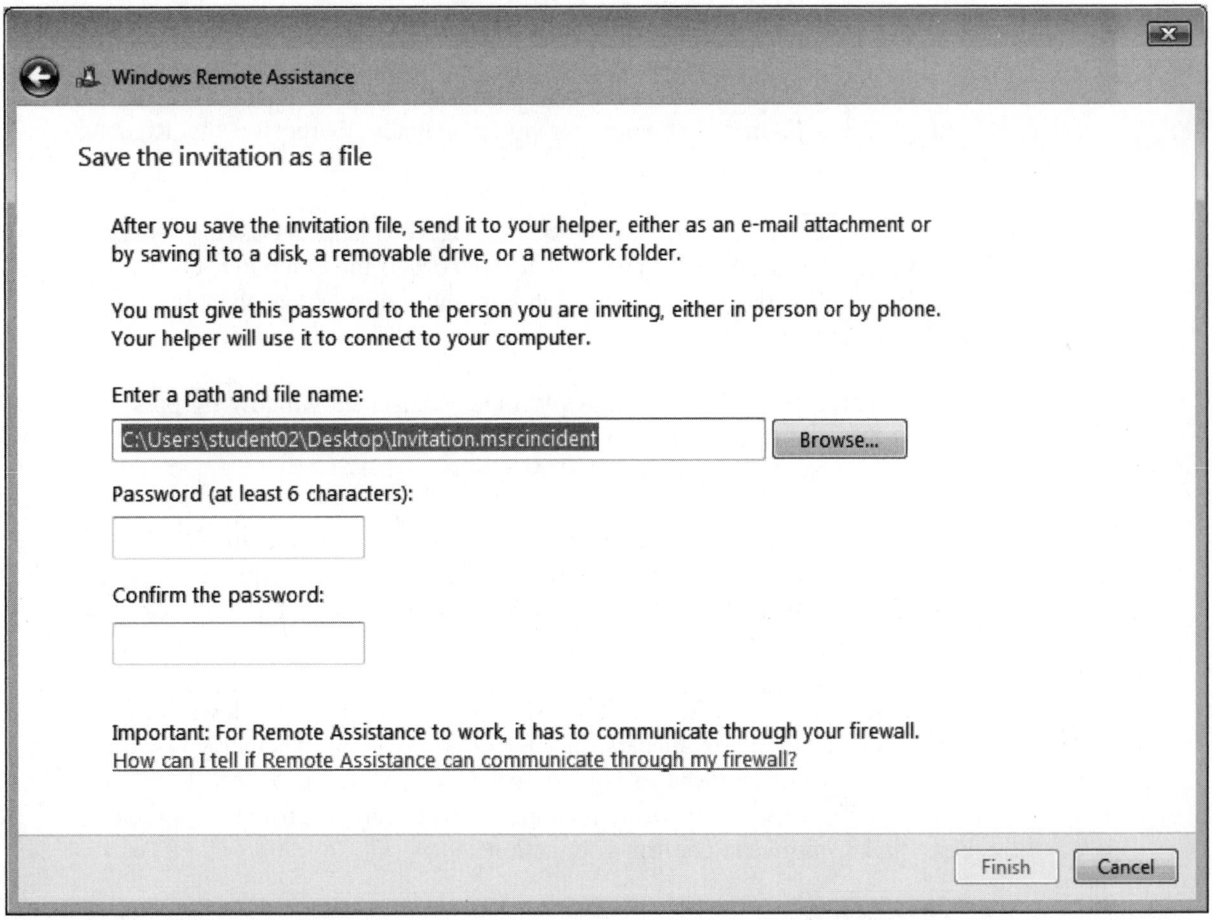

Figure 11-4
Save The Invitation As A File page

5. In the Enter A Path And File Name text box, key **\\server01\students\studentxx\Invitation.msrcIncident**.

6. Key **P@ssw0rd** in the Password and Confirm The Password text boxes, and click Finish. A Windows Remote Assistance window appears, as shown in Figure 11-5, indicating that the computer is waiting for an incoming connection.

Figure 11-5
Waiting For Incoming Connection window

7. Tell your lab partner that your computer is ready to receive the Remote Assistance connection.

8. When a Windows Remote Assistance message box appears asking whether you would like to allow your partner to connect to the computer, click Yes. The Waiting For Incoming Connection window indicates that the connection has been established.

9. Take a screen shot of the Windows Remote Assistance window by pressing Alt+Prt Scr, and then paste the resulting image into the lab11_worksheet file in the page provided by pressing Ctrl+V.

10. When your partner initiates a Chat session, a Chat interface appears in the Windows Remote Assistance window containing a message from your partner. Respond to the message by typing some text in the text box and clicking Send.

11. When your partner clicks the Request Control button, a Windows Remote Assistance message box appears on your desktop asking whether you would like to allow your partner to share control of your desktop. Select the Allow Studentxx To Respond To User Account Control Prompts checkbox and click Yes. Click Continue to confirm your action.

Question 2	What happens next?

12. Click Start, point to All Programs, and click Windows Update.

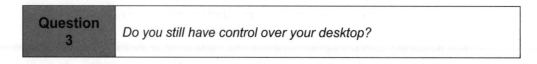

Question 3	Do you still have control over your desktop?

13. On the Windows Remote Assistance toolbar, click Send File. An Open dialog box appears.

14. Select Documents, and open the Remote Assistance Logs folder. Select a log file and click Open. Once your partner approves, the file transfer is completed.

15. On the Windows Remote Assistance toolbar, click the Pause button. On your partner's workstation, the Windows Remote Assistance window goes black.

16. When your partner clicks the Disconnect button, the connection is terminated and a message to that effect appears in your Windows Remote Assistance window, as shown in Figure 11-6. The Windows Remote Assistance window returns to the Waiting For Incoming Connection state.

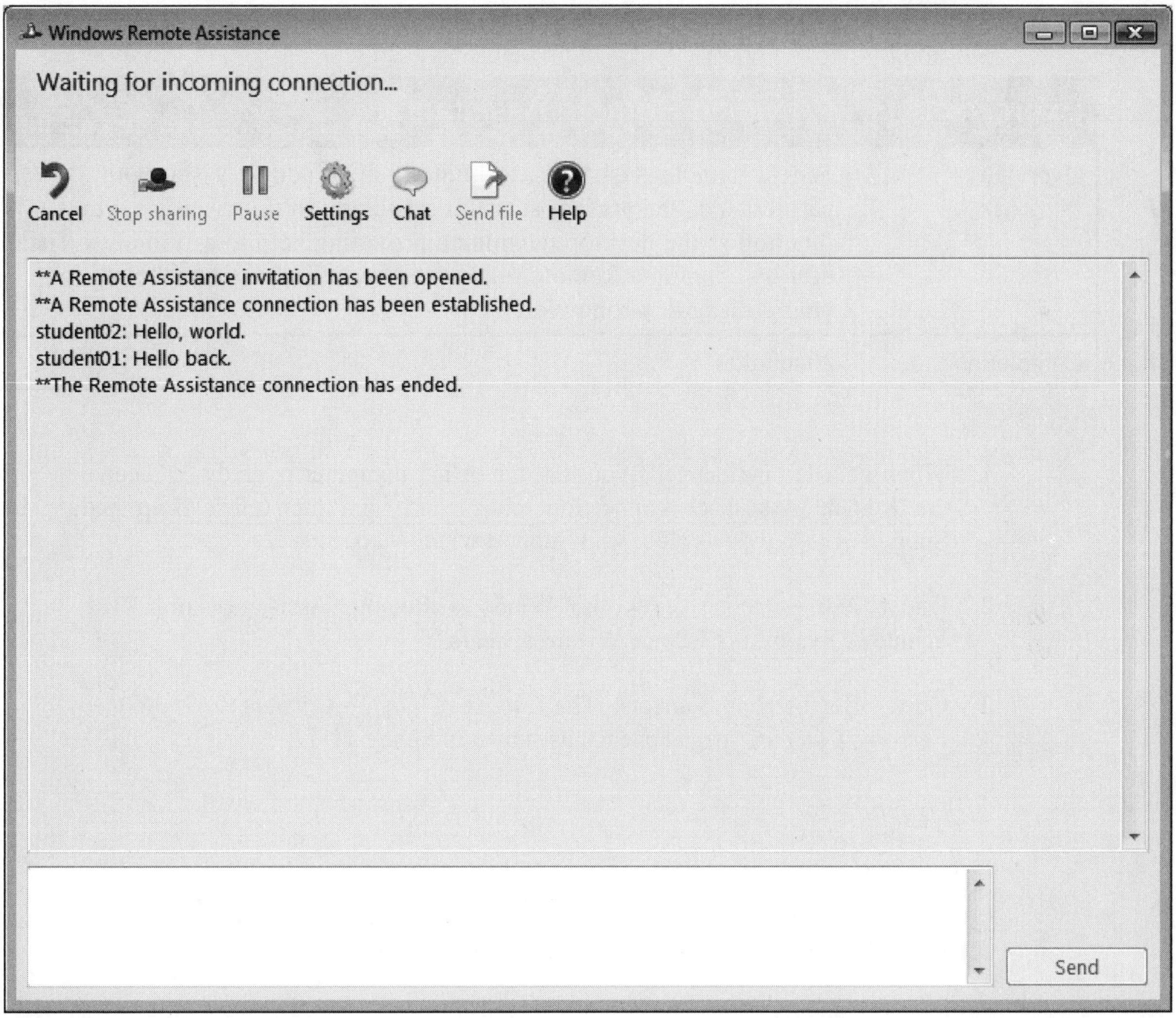

Figure 11-6
Waiting For Incoming Connection window

17. On the Windows Remote Assistance toolbar, click the Cancel button. A message box appears asking you to confirm your action.

18. Click Yes. The Windows Remote Assistance window closes, and the wizard reappears.

19. Click Cancel. The wizard closes.

20. Leave the computer logged on for the next exercise.

 NOTE *If you have not done so already, switch Remote Assistance roles with your partner and complete Exercise 11.3.*

Exercise 11.3	Providing Remote Assistance
Overview	To test Remote Assistance technology in Windows Vista, both partners must be present at their computers. In this exercise, you function as the desktop technician providing help to a Windows Vista user by opening a Remote Assistance invitation and connecting to your colleague's computer.
Completion time	30 minutes

1. When your lab partner tells you that his or her computer is ready to receive the Remote Assistance connection, click Start, and then click Help and Support. The Windows Help And Support window appears.

2. Under Ask Someone, click the Windows Remote Assistance link. The Windows Remote Assistance Wizard appears.

3. Click Offer To Help Someone. The *Choose A Way To Connect To The Other Person's Computer* page appears, as shown in Figure 11-7.

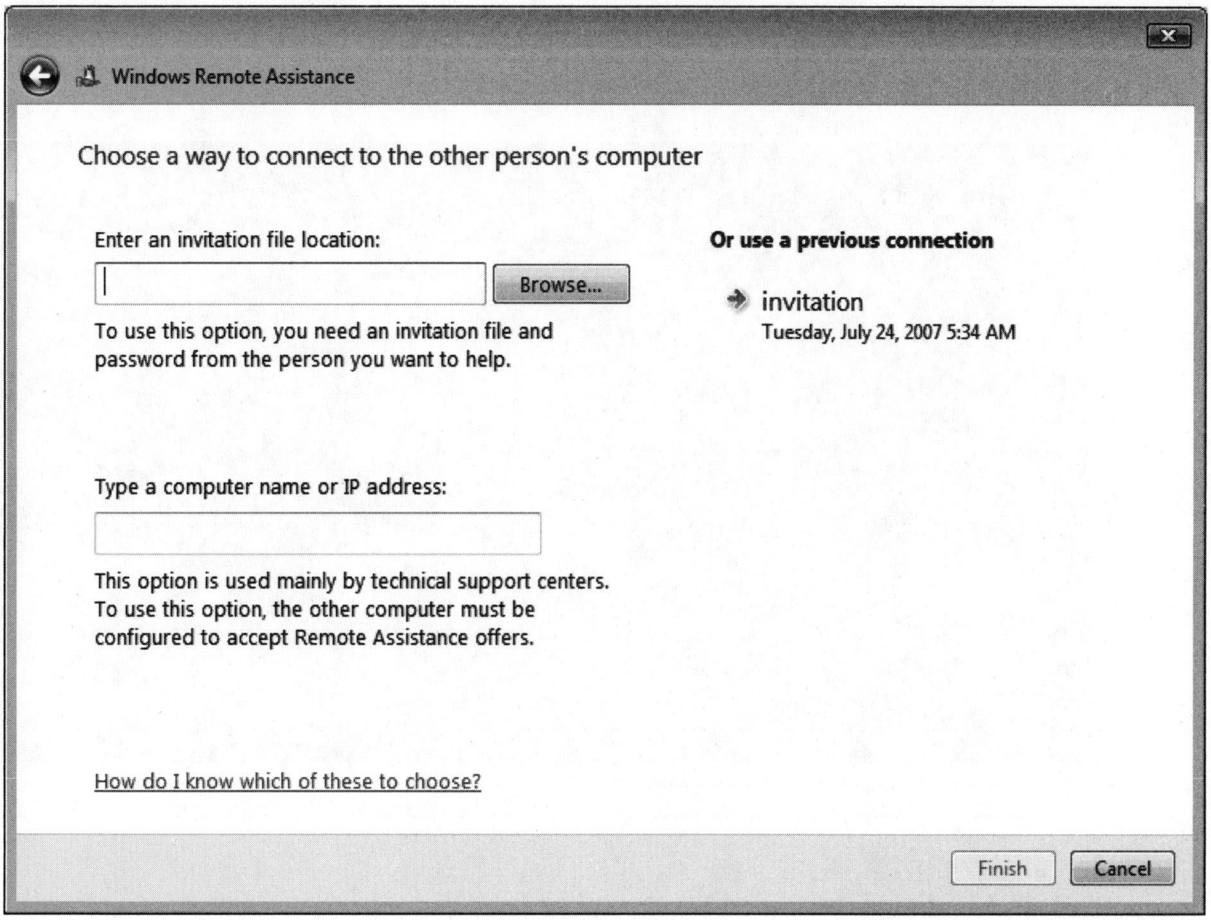

Figure 11-7
Choose A Way To Connect To The Other Person's Computer page

4. In the Enter An Invitation File Location text box, key
    \\server01\students\studentxx\Invitation.msrcIncident, where *xx* is your
    lab partner's student number, and click Finish. The *Type The Password To
    Connect To The Remote Computer* page appears.

> **NOTE**
>
> *Be sure to use your lab partner's student number in this step so that
> you open the invitation your partner created and not your own
> invitation.*

5. In the Enter Password text box, key **P@ssw0rd** and click OK.

6. A Windows Remote Assistance window appears, as shown in Figure 11-8,
    indicating that the program is waiting for acceptance from the other computer.

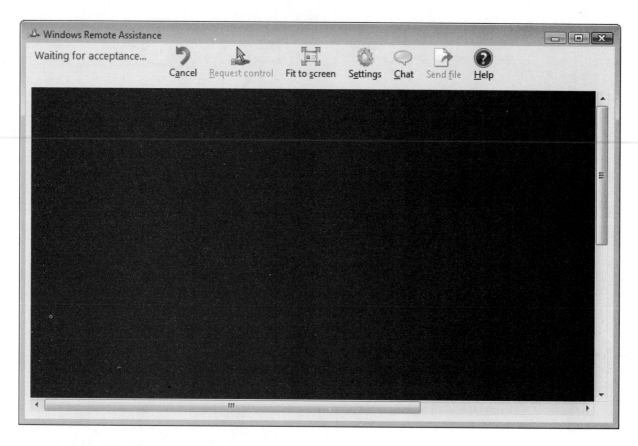

Figure 11-8
Windows Remote Assistance window

7. When your lab partner accepts the connection, the other computer's desktop appears in the Windows Remote Assistance window.

8. Take a screen shot of the Windows Remote Assistance window by pressing Alt+Prt Scr, and then paste the resulting image into the lab11_worksheet file in the page provided by pressing Ctrl+V.

9. Click the Chat button in the Windows Remote Assistance toolbar. A Chat interface appears in the Windows Remote Assistance window.

NOTE	*In this and the following steps, be sure to distinguish carefully between the elements on your desktop and those on your partner's desktop, which appear in your Remote Assistance window.*

10. Key a message to your partner in the text box, and click Send.

Question 4	*Does your partner receive the Chat message? How can you tell?*

11. Click the Chat button again to close the Chat interface.

12. Click the Start button, and open the Control Panel on your partner's desktop in the Windows Remote Assistance window.

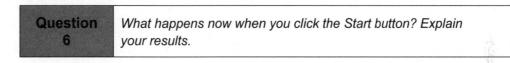

Question 5	What happens when you click the Start button? Explain your results.

13. Click the Request Control button on the Windows Remote Assistance toolbar. A Windows Remote Assistance message box appears on your partner's desktop asking whether he or she would like to allow you to share control of the desktop.

14. Once your partner agrees to share control of the desktop, try again to click the Start button and open the Control Panel.

Question 6	What happens now when you click the Start button? Explain your results.

15. Your partner will now attempt to send you a file using the Remote Assistance connection. When the Would You Like To Accept A File message box appears, click Yes.

16. A Save As dialog box appears. Click Save, and the file is transferred to your desktop.

Question 7	What happens next?

17. On the Windows Remote Assistance toolbar, click the Disconnect button. A message box appears asking you to confirm your action.

18. Click Yes. The Windows Remote Assistance window closes and the wizard reappears.

19. Click Cancel. The wizard closes.

20. Leave the computer logged on for the next exercise.

NOTE

If you have not done so already, switch Remote Assistance roles with your partner and complete Exercise 11.2.

Exercise 11.4   Connecting with Remote Desktop

Overview	Remote Desktop technology in Windows Vista does not require a user to be present at the remote computer. In this exercise, you and your colleague take turns connecting to each others' computers and controlling them from a remote location.
Completion time	30 minutes

1. Ask your partner to log off his or her computer while you perform this exercise.

2. Log on (if necessary) using the Student## account, where xx is your student number, and the password **P@ssw0rd**.

3. Click Start. Point to All Programs > Accessories, and click Remote Desktop Connection. The Remote Desktop Connection window appears.

4. Click Options. The Remote Desktop Connection window expands.

5. On the General tab in the Computer text box, key **Computer*xx***, where *xx* is the number of your partner's computer.

6. Click the Display tab, and set the Remote Desktop Size to a resolution smaller than that of your computer.

7. Click the Local Resources tab, and clear the Printers checkbox.

8. Click the More button. The Local Devices And Resources dialog box appears.

9. Select the Drives checkbox, as shown in Figure 11-9, and click OK.

Figure 11-9
Local Devices And Resources dialog box

10. Click the Experience tab and, from the drop-down list, select LAN (10 Mbps or Higher).

11. Click Connect. A Windows Security dialog box appears.

12. Enter your logon credentials using your Student*xx* user name and the password **P@ssw0rd**, and click OK. The Do You Trust The Computer You Are Connecting To? dialog box appears.

13. Select the Don't Prompt Me Again For Connections To This Computer checkbox and click Yes.

14. A Computer*xx* Remote Desktop window appears, containing an image of the remote computer's desktop.

15. Take a screen shot of the Computer*xx* Remote Desktop window by pressing Alt+Prt Scr, and then paste the resulting image into the lab11_worksheet file in the page provided by pressing Ctrl+V.

16. In the Computer*xx* Remote Desktop window, close the Welcome Center window.

17. In the Computer*xx* Remote Desktop window, click Start and open the Control Panel.

18. In the Computer*xx* Remote Desktop window, Click System And Maintenance, and then click Windows Update. The Windows Update control panel appears.

19. In the Computer*xx* Remote Desktop window, click Change Settings. The *Choose How Windows Can Install Updates* page appears.

20. In the Computer*xx* Remote Desktop window, select the Download Updates But Let Me Choose Whether To Install Them option. Then, select the Include Recommended Updates When Downloading, Installing, Or Notifying Me About Updates checkbox and click OK.

21. In the Computer*xx* Remote Desktop window, click Continue to confirm your action.

22. In the Computer*xx* Remote Desktop window, click the Start menu, and then click the Disconnect ("X") button. The Computer*xx* Remote Desktop window closes.

23. Log off of the computer.

LAB REVIEW QUESTIONS

Completion time	10 minutes

1. What happens if someone attempts to use an invitation to initiate a Remote Assistance connection to another computer when there is no user present at that other computer?

2. During a Remote Desktop session in which you are accessing a computer on your network, if you launch a program in your Remote desktop window, which computer's processor and memory are used to run the program?

3. During a Remote Assistance or Remote Desktop session, what would happen if you opened the Network Connections window on the remote computer and configured the network adapter to use a different IP address?

LAB CHALLENGE: REMOTELY CONFIGURING WINDOWS UPDATE

Completion time	20 minutes

Your IT director is planning to install Windows Server Update Services (WSUS) on the Server01 computer. Active Directory has not been deployed on the network as of yet, so the IT staff will have to configure each computer to obtain updates from the WSUS server individually. Using the computers in the test deployment, your task is to develop a procedure that will enable the IT staff to remotely configure a Windows Vista computer to automatically download and install all critical and recommended updates obtained from the WSUS server every day at 5:00 AM. To complete this challenge, write out the steps of the procedure.

LAB 12
TROUBLESHOOTING WINDOWS VISTA

This lab contains the following exercises and activities:

Exercise 12.1   Troubleshooting Network Connectivity

Exercise 12.2   Troubleshooting Disk Access

Exercise 12.3   Troubleshooting Shared Folders

Exercise 12.4   Troubleshooting the Desktop

Exercise 12.5   Troubleshooting Logon Problems

BEFORE YOU BEGIN

This lab consists of five computing scenarios in which you play the role of a help desk technician who is required to troubleshoot problems reported by Windows Vista users. Your instructor has configured each of the Windows Vista workstations in the classroom to malfunction in some way, and it is your job, based on the information in each scenario, to diagnose the problem and solve it. Each of the computers in the classroom has been marked with a number from 1 to 5. To complete each scenario, you must go to a workstation bearing the same number as the exercise, start the clean copy of Windows Vista installed in Lab 3, log on using the Student*xx* account for that computer (using the password **P@ssw0rd**), and troubleshoot the problem described in the scenario using only the tools provided with the operating system. The problem could be hardware- or software-related, but in none of the scenarios will it be necessary to open the computer case.

In this lab, the process is just as important as the results. As you work with each computer, you must keep a detailed troubleshooting paper log that includes everything you checked, everything you found, and everything you did. Keep detailed notes regarding the tools you used, how you used them, and the results of your tests. Once you have arrived at a solution to the problem described in the scenario, document the exact procedure for repairing the system in your log. Do not share your work with other students. Finally, you must return the computer to the same state in which you found it and shut the computer down. In other words, after fixing each computer, you must break it again so that another student can troubleshoot the same problem on it. When you have completed all five troubleshooting scenarios, submit your logs to your instructor.

SCENARIO

You are a desktop technician for Contoso, Ltd., working at the Windows Vista help desk. When a user calls or emails you with a computer problem, it is your job to travel to that user's workstation and resolve it. To account for your time and to build up a company troubleshooting database, you must document each of your calls as well as the troubleshooting process for each computer on which you work.

After completing this lab, you will be able to:

■ Troubleshoot a variety of Windows Vista configuration problems

Estimated lab time: 125 minutes

Exercise 12.1	Troubleshooting Network Connectivity
Overview	Rob calls the help desk to report that he cannot access any Websites on the Internet. While he is still on the phone, you have him try to access a file on his departmental server. In both cases, his attempts fail. Troubleshoot Rob's computer and determine why he is unable to access the network. The troubleshooting process will be completed when you are able to access the network using Rob's computer.
Completion time	25 minutes

Exercise 12.2	Troubleshooting Disk Access
Overview	Alice sends an email to the help desk stating that when she tried to copy some files to her X: drive, which is a volume on her local hard disk, she was unable to do so. Because Alice has already left for her vacation, she cannot provide any more details about the problem, but she writes that she would appreciate the problem being fixed by the time she returns. The troubleshooting process will be completed when Alice can write files to her X: drive.
Completion time	25 minutes

Exercise 12.3	Troubleshooting Shared Folders
Overview	Gail is the head bookkeeper for your company, and she stores the firm's financial spreadsheet files on her Windows Vista computer. The other bookkeepers in the department, who all have user accounts that are members of the Users group, work with the spreadsheets on Gail's computer by accessing two shared folders called Payable and Receivable. Gail has just called the help desk and reported that since having a new network adapter installed, the other bookkeepers have been unable to access the shares. However, Gail is able to access Websites on the Internet. The troubleshooting process will be completed when other computers on the network are able to read files from and write them to the Payable and Receivable shares on Gail's computer.
Completion time	25 minutes

Exercise 12.4	Troubleshooting the Desktop
Overview	Harold has been away on vacation for two weeks, during which time a temp has been working at his desk and using his computer. On his first day back, Harold starts his computer and logs on normally, but finds that the taskbar is missing from his desktop. He calls the help desk, and you travel to Harold's office to fix the problem. The troubleshooting process will be completed when the Harold's taskbar is accessible.
Completion time	25 minutes

Exercise 12.5	Troubleshooting Logon Problems
Overview	Sarah calls the help desk because she has an intermittent problem logging on to her computer. Some mornings, she logs on without a problem. On other days, she cannot log on at first, but after waiting a few minutes, her logon is successful. This morning, it took three attempts over the course of 30 minutes before she was able to log on, and she is becoming extremely frustrated. The troubleshooting process will be completed when Sarah is able to log on to her computer consistently with no delays.
Completion time	25 minutes

NOTES

NOTES

NOTES

NOTES

NOTES

NOTES

NOTES

NOTES

NOTES

NOTES

NOTES

NOTES